REVISED FIRST EDITION

SMARTER WRITING:
A STUDENT'S GUIDE TO COLLEGE COMPOSITION AND RESEARCH

by Yelena Kajevic Bailey-Kirby

cognella® | ACADEMIC PUBLISHING

Bassim Hamadeh, CEO and Publisher

Carrie Montoya, Manager, Revisions and Author Care

Kaela Martin, Project Editor

Alia Bales, Associate Production Editor

Jess Estrella, Senior Graphic Designer

Natalie Lakosil, Licensing Manager

Joyce Lue, Interior Designer

Natalie Piccotti, Senior Marketing Manager

Kassie Graves, Director of Acquisitions and Sales

Jamie Giganti, Senior Managing Editor

cognella® | ACADEMIC PUBLISHING

Contents

CHAPTER 1
THESIS, INTRODUCTION, BODY, AND CONCLUSION

Figure 1.1   Thesis Statement Cartoon

In this chapter, you will learn to write a clear thesis as well as develop an introduction, body paragraphs, and conclusion for your essays. You always need to state a clear thesis in every essay assigned to you, and you will need to organize your ideas with an introduction, body paragraphs, and conclusion.

Therefore, you will practice distinguishing between statements that are too broad, too narrow, two quite separate reasons, or even simply an announcement before reviewing how to formulate a clear thesis statement from the sample templates. Then you will review the steps for organizing your essays with a sequence of practice activities on developing the paragraphs of your essay.

THESIS

WHAT IS THESIS?

Thesis means a statement that declares the main ideas, position of your paper, and purpose that you plan to emphasize in your essay. In other words, it is a precisely worded assertion that provides a conjecture about the subject matter that your research can defend, and it usually expresses the method you will take with your material. Hence, a thesis must be more than just an announcement of your subject, a statement of fact, a title, or a broad claim, and it should not include abstract words like *society* or *culture* and vague words such as *interesting*, *difficult*, or *unusual*.

WHERE CAN YOU FIND A PROVOCATIVE THESIS?

To find a provocative thesis, you may need to start with a brainstorming list by identifying several issues that interest you and determining what is open to debate. For instance, you might record something like the following examples: Animal Poaching, Human Trafficking, Deforestation, and so on. After you have jotted down a few ideas, consider freewriting for five

Practice Activity A: Before you can develop a stimulating thesis, you must apply inquiry to generate ideas on a topic in the following three steps: reflect, reassess, and recognize. You might need to read some articles with opposing viewpoints before you take a position on a controversial topic or even propose a few journalistic questions to sharpen your focus on the subject. Follow the three steps to inquiry listed below, and then you will share your response with your peers and instructor during a class discussion. (See the example below that approaches inquiry on the topic of animal testing to help you get started.)

1. REFLECT: Reflect upon the different points of view on your topic and determine the root of your interest on this subject.
2. REASSESS: Reassess what is the actual debate on your topic by devising a question.
3. RECOGNIZE: Recognize your readers' needs, backgrounds, and biases by considering what you want to teach them.

An Example of the Three Steps to Inquiry:
1. Reflect: I want to know how animal testing has had harmful consequences on humans and the animals being used in these experiments because I am a vegan who does not want any cruelty to come to animals.
2. Reassess: To what degree are there more humane and successful alternatives to animal testing that can be used to advance medicine and save lives by replacing the cruel experiments still practiced today?
3. Recognize: How much do my readers know about animal testing, and what new information can I share with them?

to ten minutes by exploring one of your topics from different points of view and explaining the reasons for your curiosity about the issue and what knowledge you already have about it.

Afterward, ask some journalistic questions of who, what, where, when, why, and how in order to generate more ideas to help you discover what is at the heart of a controversial topic or a popular debate in the media that you still need to learn. In other words, pursue questions that demand proof through research and facts as well as encourage creative and critical thinking.

You will want to produce thought-provoking questions that ask who is responsible or what is a major influence behind the circumstances, raise awareness about a problem, evaluate if there is a solution, determine a call to action as a preventative measure, identify a change of policy that might be a remedy to the problem, evaluate the cause of a certain crisis, and/or address the intentions behind one group over another on a controversial dilemma. By the end of this process of inquiry, you will need to recognize your readers and their concerns, backgrounds, and biases as well.

HOW DO YOU AVOID COMMON ERRORS WHEN FORMULATING A THESIS?

In order to avoid common errors when formulating a thesis, you must avoid simply announcing your topic or just stating a title for the subject of your essay. You also want to avoid writing too broad of a statement that is actually too extensive in scope to cover in a few pages of an essay assignment. On the other hand, you do not want to state a fact that would end up being too

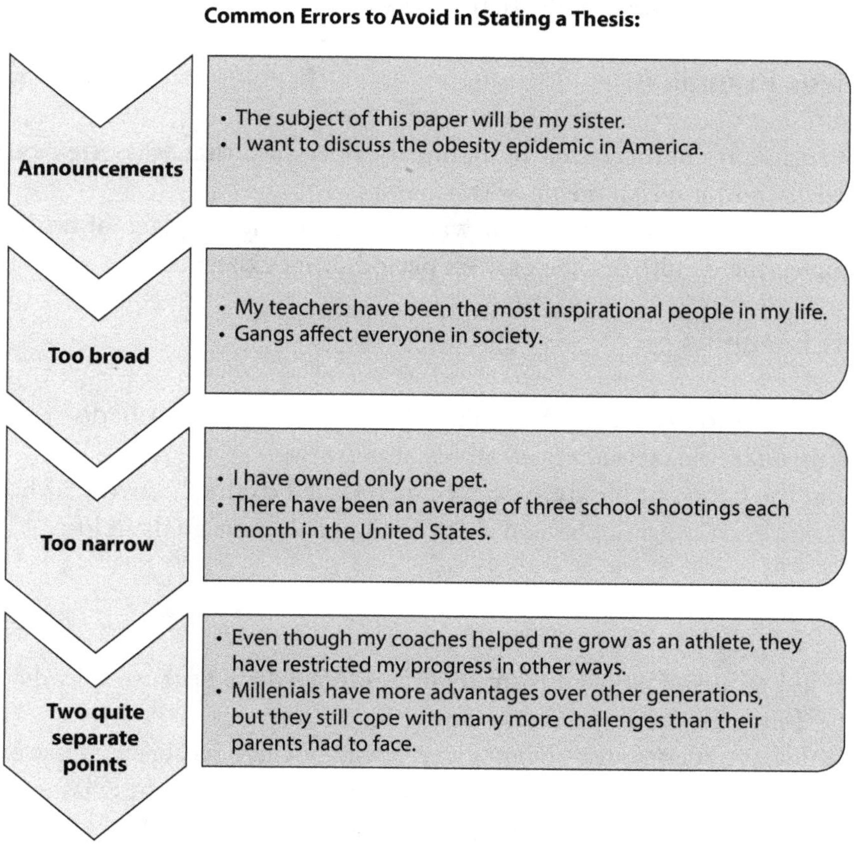

Common Errors to Avoid in Stating a Thesis:

Announcements
- The subject of this paper will be my sister.
- I want to discuss the obesity epidemic in America.

Too broad
- My teachers have been the most inspirational people in my life.
- Gangs affect everyone in society.

Too narrow
- I have owned only one pet.
- There have been an average of three school shootings each month in the United States.

Two quite separate points
- Even though my coaches helped me grow as an athlete, they have restricted my progress in other ways.
- Millenials have more advantages over other generations, but they still cope with many more challenges than their parents had to face.

Figure 1.2

narrow and limiting for a paper. Besides these types of errors, you need to steer clear of claiming two quite separate points for a thesis because this usually results in a contradiction of your key points. Here are a few examples to help you understand the different pitfalls and how to sidestep them.

WHAT ARE SOME EXAMPLES OF A CLEAR THESIS?

Formulating a clear thesis can depend on the type of essay that your instructor assigns. For instance, your goal might be to clarify the object or process of your subject by breaking it down into its separate elements in an analytical paper, while for an expository paper you might need to inform readers about a new topic with explanations, details, and descriptions.

However, your instructor might require you to take a stance on a debatable issue, make a claim about it, and support your opinion with evidence that includes facts, statistics, and/or other research material for an argument paper. Listed below are some examples of clearly worded statements for different types of essays that you might be asked to write.

Notice how these thesis statements provide a clear focus on their topic and communicate their intentions about the subject that will be discussed in the paper. Other shared traits below include statements connected loosely by coordinating conjunctions (i.e., FANBOYS: *for, and, nor, but, or, yet, so*) or subordinating conjunctions (i.e., *although, because, since, through*) that indicate a relationship between the ideas in the sentences. Then, you will be asked to complete the practice activity on thesis statements that follows.

Expository Thesis Examples

- The Stalin regime is characterized by political oppression that was often carried out with extreme cruelty and imprisonment of the masses.
- Stonehenge excavations suggest that it was a multifunctional place of healing for the sick and worship of the dead from the earliest period of its existence.

Analysis Thesis Examples

- A careful examination of Edgar Allan Poe's "The Cask of Amontillado" reveals the theme of revenge through the characters, symbols, and irony.
- Investigating the habits of highly successful people led to the discovery of how rising early and meditating each morning helped them accomplish their goals in life.

Argumentative Thesis Examples

- Parents should remove fast food from their children's diets because it leads to preventable health issues, such as obesity and diabetes.
- Since students have become too reliant on technology, there has been an increase in memory loss, mood disorders, and loneliness, and teachers can alleviate these issues by minimizing a student's usage of technology in the classroom.

Checklist for Stating a Clear Thesis:

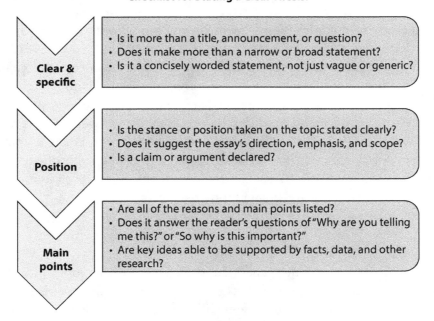

Figure 1.3

Practice Activity B: Identify which of the following statements are (A) an announcement, (B) too broad, (C) too narrow, (D) two quite separate points, or (E) a clear thesis.

1. My first job was babysitting.
2. The president has changed our society.
3. This essay will discuss the people that you meet in college.
4. My girlfriend and I are similar in temperament, but we have quite different interests when it comes to hobbies.
5. Anyone who plans to lose weight must exercise regularly, control his or her meal portions, and drink at least eight glasses of water daily.
6. Technology has made Americans lazy.
7. I am going to write about human trafficking.
8. My last trip was to New York, but most Americans prefer to travel to Hawaii.
9. The way our society treats immigrants is unfair.
10. After earning an F on the exam, I realized that I needed to get a tutor, join a study group, and take better notes during class.

HOW DO I DEVELOP A CLEAR AND MORE COMPLEX THESIS STATEMENT?

Before you write a clear and complex thesis statement, you should generate ideas by using the journalistic questions suggested in Practice Activity A in this chapter. Once you are ready to formulate a thesis, remember you want to state it early in the essay, within the introduction paragraph.

Foremost, you want to establish if your issue is recent and significant enough, review others' key arguments and data about the issue in the past, and address any misconceptions or discrepancies in the information examined and produced by others. Now, you will practice writing a thesis by following the templates listed below. The templates will help you create a compelling thesis with clarity and concise language. You can also replace any of the subordinate clauses, words, and verbs provided in the templates by using a thesaurus, or you can even interchange scholars, experts, scientists, writers, and researchers with other subjects.

Practice Activity C: If you have not generated ideas for a possible topic, please complete Practice Activity A in this chapter before you formulate three possible thesis statements below. When you have completed them, you will share them with your peers and instructor during a class discussion. Your peers and instructor may offer suggestions to clarify your position or modify a reason that you may want to explore further in an essay.

An example for creating a thesis from the templates below:

Even though some experts have insisted animal testing is necessary to advance medicine, **_they have overlooked the evidence that confirms_** animals are treated inhumanely, alternative methods exist, and experimental methods are often incompatible to a human beings' physiology.

Complex Thesis Statements

1. Although many scholars contend (interpret, maintain, claim) _____, new evidence proves (suggests, recommends, determines) that _____ is the best course of action (solution, truth, reality).
2. Even though some experts have considered (deemed, judged, insisted) _____, they have overlooked (ignored, disregarded) the evidence (proof, data, facts) that propose/s (indicate/s, confirm/s) _____.
3. Because some researchers concur (accept, agree, conform) with/to the idea of _____, it is vital (beneficial, essential) to examine (expand, limit, enhance) one's understanding of the issue with _____.

INTRODUCTION

WHAT IS AN INTRODUCTION?

An introduction is the opening paragraph to your essay. It establishes the subject of your essay to readers, and it should provide some background that directs the reader to your thesis statement. The introduction can also be used to grab readers' attention and shape their opinions about your topic.

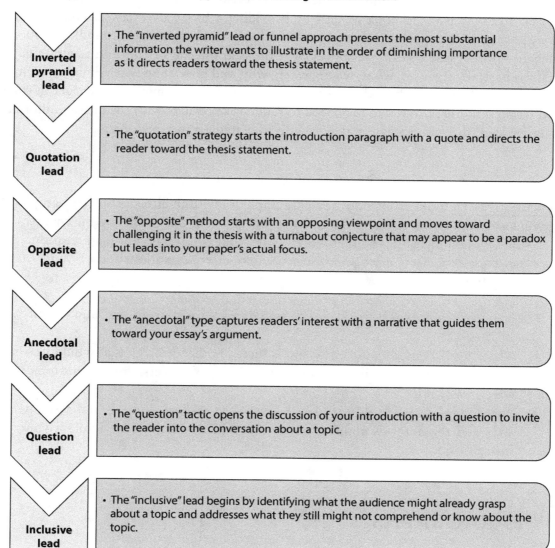

Six Approaches to Writing an Introduction:

Inverted pyramid lead
- The "inverted pyramid" lead or funnel approach presents the most substantial information the writer wants to illustrate in the order of diminishing importance as it directs readers toward the thesis statement.

Quotation lead
- The "quotation" strategy starts the introduction paragraph with a quote and directs the reader toward the thesis statement.

Opposite lead
- The "opposite" method starts with an opposing viewpoint and moves toward challenging it in the thesis with a turnabout conjecture that may appear to be a paradox but leads into your paper's actual focus.

Anecdotal lead
- The "anecdotal" type captures readers' interest with a narrative that guides them toward your essay's argument.

Question lead
- The "question" tactic opens the discussion of your introduction with a question to invite the reader into the conversation about a topic.

Inclusive lead
- The "inclusive" lead begins by identifying what the audience might already grasp about a topic and addresses what they still might not comprehend or know about the topic.

Figure 1.4

HOW SHOULD YOU BEGIN AN INTRODUCTION?

There are several ways to approach the beginning of an introduction that are used by journalists; these are called "leads." You may consider engaging your readers with a story (**anecdotal lead**), or you may want to invite your audience to participate in the conversation by asking a significant question (**question lead**) about your topic.

While still another option may be to offer a surprising statistic or fact to pique your audience's interest and curiosity, you may need to include a quote (**quotation lead**) from an expert to establish your credibility on the issue from the start. Alternatively, you may want to speculate about the possible outcomes and how they might affect your audience in the long term by addressing the opposing side's assumptions before you reveal your actual claims (**opposite lead**).

However, you may want to hook readers by providing a broad overview of concepts or a summary about the main points (**inverted pyramid lead**)—including background, definitions, or the debate—of the issue before you state a clear thesis at the end of your introduction paragraph. This is basically the who, what, where, when, why, and how of an issue. Finally, you may recognize that your audience's knowledge of certain areas of a topic might be stronger in some ways and weaker in others, and you may need to familiarize readers with the missing information (**inclusive lead**) that you recognize they lack to fully understand the topic.

Practice Activity D: Write an introduction paragraph or revise an introduction paragraph that you have already written for an essay by applying one of the leads from the chapter. When you have completed it, you will share it with your peers and your instructor during a class discussion. Your peers and instructor may offer suggestions for a rewrite of your introduction. Here are three questions that you and your peers will need to answer:

1. To what degree was a thesis clearly stated? Explain your answer, and identify the thesis.
2. What "lead" is used in the essay and is there another strategy that would have been more engaging or better suited for initiating a conversation on this topic? Why or why not?
3. Does the introduction differentiate between the audience's needs and assumptions and the author's ability to offer a compelling argument? Explain your answer.

BODY PARAGRAPHS

WHAT IS THE BODY OF AN ESSAY?

Each body paragraph is organized according to the main points from your thesis statement. The body paragraphs are situated between the introduction and conclusion, and they offer evidence, proof, and support for your stance with a well-developed discussion.

Three Stages of Drafting Effective Body Paragraphs:

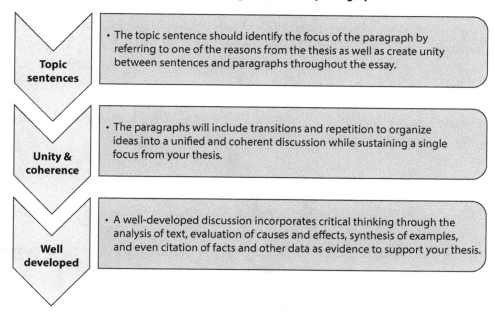

Figure 1.5

HOW SHOULD YOU WRITE YOUR BODY PARAGRAPHS?

The body paragraphs may be arranged by themes (**thematic**), grouped by comparisons between two or more elements (**contrasting**), relay questions one after another (**sequential**), or even deal with an issue from earliest event or cause to most recent (**chronological**). However, the most important factors to include in a body paragraph are examples, facts, and discussions on your topic to support your thesis while crediting data with a parenthetical citation for any sources that you quote, paraphrase, and/or summarize. Hence, whenever you integrate information from sources, you should explain the meaning and relevance of its data in supporting your thesis as well.

You will mainly develop your body paragraphs with critical strategies like analyzing texts, evaluating the relationship between causes and outcomes, defining terms, and making comparisons. Body paragraphs should also contain sentences that directly relate back to the main idea of the topic sentence (first sentence of your paragraph), since the topic sentence usually refers to one of your reasons from the thesis statement. The topic sentences operate as a signpost to direct readers toward the next logical point from your thesis as well as the question motivating the argument of your paper.

Along with a well-developed discussion and unity, you should create smooth-flowing connections between your ideas. For instance, you may need to use transitions to indicate comparisons (i.e., *Similarly, Likewise, Also*) or contrasting points (i.e., *On the other hand, However, Conversely*). In other cases, you may want to link information in tiers with *Moreover, Furthermore*, and *As a result*. Other ways to create coherence consist of repeating key words to carry concepts from one sentence to another or using pronouns that convey significant nouns from a previous sentence.

Continued

Practice Activity E: Draft a five-paragraph outline like the sample provided below to help you organize your thoughts before you begin drafting actual body paragraphs on a subject that you generated earlier in this chapter's practice exercise, unless your instructor has or will assign specific topics. Once you have written at least one well-developed body paragraph or the entire rough draft of your essay, you will share it with your peers and instructor, who will offer some suggestions during a class discussion. Answer the following questions with your peers:

1. To what degree does each body paragraph apply critical-thinking strategies (i.e., comparisons, analysis, synthesis, etc.)?
2. What examples are provided as proof, if any, to support the thesis argument?
3. Are sources and data cited as connections are being made?
4. Does each paragraph offer a logical order for the ideas while creating coherence and unity between sentences? If so, how? If not, what is missing?

Sample Outline

I. Introduction (Thesis)

II. First Point/Reason
    A. Provide Evidence/Cite Data
    B. Explain/Evaluate Support

III. Second Point/Reason
    A. Provide Evidence/Cite Data
    B. Explain/Evaluate Support

IV. Third Point/Reason
    A. Provide Evidence/Cite Data
    B. Explain/Evaluate Support

V. Conclusion

CONCLUSION

WHAT IS A CONCLUSION?

The conclusion is the final paragraph of your paper. It reasserts the main claim from your thesis and summarizes the main points of your essay. It does not bring in new material or data that you

Five Approaches to Writing a Conclusion:

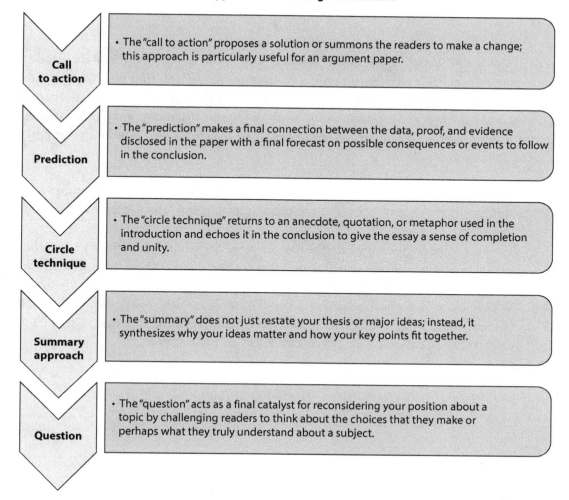

Call to action
- The "call to action" proposes a solution or summons the readers to make a change; this approach is particularly useful for an argument paper.

Prediction
- The "prediction" makes a final connection between the data, proof, and evidence disclosed in the paper with a final forecast on possible consequences or events to follow in the conclusion.

Circle technique
- The "circle technique" returns to an anecdote, quotation, or metaphor used in the introduction and echoes it in the conclusion to give the essay a sense of completion and unity.

Summary approach
- The "summary" does not just restate your thesis or major ideas; instead, it synthesizes why your ideas matter and how your key points fit together.

Question
- The "question" acts as a final catalyst for reconsidering your position about a topic by challenging readers to think about the choices that they make or perhaps what they truly understand about a subject.

Figure 1.6

did not discuss earlier in the paper; instead, it aims to recap the key ideas of your paper with an insightful and memorable closure.

HOW SHOULD YOU APPROACH YOUR CONCLUSION?

There are several ways to wrap up your essay and leave your reader with a lasting impression. You may end your conclusion with a **prediction** about possible outcomes and consequences, or you may choose to challenge readers with a **call to action** and offer them a solution to a problem. Moreover, you may refer to a provocative anecdote, quotation, or analogy with the **circle technique** to leave your readers with a newfound understanding by reminding them of an earlier example from the introduction.

You also want to leave your readers glad that they read your paper; thus, it is helpful to review the main points of your essay, reiterate your thesis, and answer "So what?" by the end of your paper with the simple **summary** approach by demonstrating why your position and argument matter. However, posing a **question** in the conclusion can also prompt readers to rethink their beliefs or lead to some introspection and further inquiry about the issue.

Practice Activity F: Write a conclusion paragraph by using one of the methods listed in this chapter, or you are welcome to revise a conclusion paragraph that you have already written for an essay. When you have completed it, you will share it with your peers and your instructor during a class discussion. Your peers and instructor may offer suggestions for a rewrite of your conclusion. Here are three questions that you and your peers will need to answer:

1. Has the conclusion reiterated the main points of the essay without simply restating the thesis and offered a convincing insight into the topic? Explain your answer.
2. To what degree does the conclusion answer "So what?" sufficiently? In other words, explain how the conclusion answers the question, "Why is this an important issue in the world today?".
3. Which of the five approaches from the chapter were used in the conclusion and is there another approach that would have tied everything together to make the essay more persuasive and appealing? Explain your answer.

CHAPTER 2
SUMMARY, PARAPHRASE, AND QUOTES

Figure 2.1   The Art of Summarizing, Paraphrasing, and Quoting Cartoon

In this chapter, you will learn about summarizing, paraphrasing, and quoting when you integrate sources in your papers. You may need to incorporate a source in your paper's discussion in order to support your thesis, support your premise, oppose your claims, or juxtapose your claims. Whether you summarize, paraphrase, and/or quote, you must always make sure that you credit your sources properly. The next chapter will review how to credit your sources with a parenthetical citation as well as in the Works Cited in MLA format and avoid plagiarism in your papers.

SUMMARY

WHAT IS SUMMARY?

Summary means you write a brief restatement of the main ideas from another author's work. You place the general ideas of the passage—such as material taken from a set of paragraphs, a chapter, an article, a poem, or even an entire book—in your own words. Basically, the best summary aims to be brief, complete, and objective when identifying the central concepts and purpose of a passage.

WHO BENEFITS FROM USING SUMMARY?

Summary can help you determine if you understand the material you have read. Presenting the ideas in a piece of writing in your own words forces you to think about what you read, and it aids you in writing more clearly, concisely, and coherently. Moreover, you become a more attentive and active reader as you examine a text and differentiate between another author's main points and subpoints as well as his or her examples, definitions, illustrations, and counterarguments in order to inform readers about the key points and purpose of a passage.

By demonstrating your knowledge of a subject through summary, you and your readers both benefit because you might be familiarizing your readers with a topic foreign to them, distinguishing the debate between two parties over a controversial issue in the media, and/or acquainting others with the plot of a new story, in order to comprehend the meaning and implications of the subject being discussed in your paper with more ease and interest. As a result, you both gain new insight into the subject as you aid readers in grasping the central points of a reading.

WHEN DO YOU WRITE A SUMMARY?

You might be asked to write a summary of an event, plot of a story, or process during an essay exam. In other cases, you might need to summarize opposing arguments or evidence for a persuasive type of essay, while in most academic writing, you might need to recapitulate main ideas before composing a paper that involves analysis, synthesis, critique, and/or research. However, summary is applied in the workplace just as often.

For instance, you may need to record meeting minutes, procedures, company policies, and/or expenses for business plans, marketing proposals, reports, letters, or interoffice memos. In other fields, you may need to reiterate key points for political bills, scientific studies, and news reports; or you may need to review the facts of a case and other evidence in a legal brief, while medical practitioners need to enter their patients' information in medical charts.

HOW DO YOU WRITE A SUMMARY?

To write a summary, you must first read critically and carefully. In other words, you will make annotations in the margins; highlight, circle, or underline main ideas or terms; and divide the reading into sections. Then, you will record the gist of the reading by condensing peripheral points down to an approximate length of one-fourth of the original passage. Here are the steps to writing a strong summary:

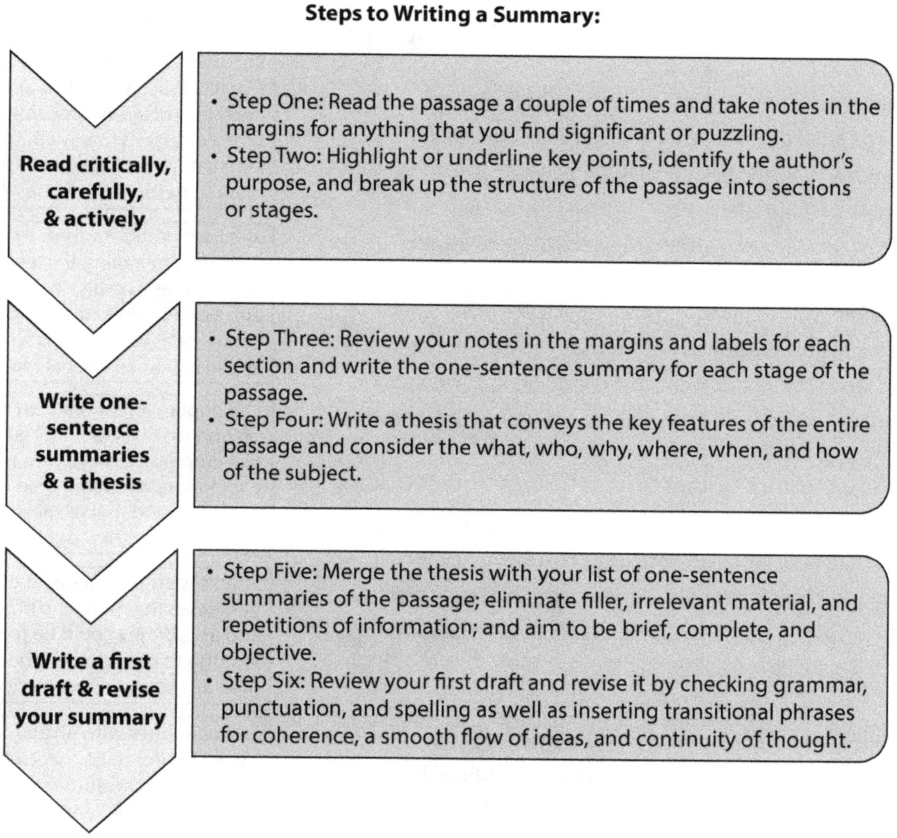

Steps to Writing a Summary:

Read critically, carefully, & actively

- Step One: Read the passage a couple of times and take notes in the margins for anything that you find significant or puzzling.
- Step Two: Highlight or underline key points, identify the author's purpose, and break up the structure of the passage into sections or stages.

Write one-sentence summaries & a thesis

- Step Three: Review your notes in the margins and labels for each section and write the one-sentence summary for each stage of the passage.
- Step Four: Write a thesis that conveys the key features of the entire passage and consider the what, who, why, where, when, and how of the subject.

Write a first draft & revise your summary

- Step Five: Merge the thesis with your list of one-sentence summaries of the passage; eliminate filler, irrelevant material, and repetitions of information; and aim to be brief, complete, and objective.
- Step Six: Review your first draft and revise it by checking grammar, punctuation, and spelling as well as inserting transitional phrases for coherence, a smooth flow of ideas, and continuity of thought.

Figure 2.2

In the following example, annotations of "Ain't I a Woman?" by Sojourner Truth have been provided around the text, and a chart follows with one-sentence summaries of her speech, with a thesis and the final draft of the summary of this text. Afterward, you will be asked to practice these steps and write a summary of Abraham Lincoln's "Emancipation Proclamation."

Sojourner Truth (1797-1883): Ain't I A Woman?
Delivered in 1851 at the Women's Convention, Akron, Ohio

She addresses the audience as "children" to create an intimate connection and establish trust as a parent who cares for their well-being in arguing for equal rights.

First Section

Well, children, where there is so much racket there must be something out of kilter. I think that 'twixt the negroes of the South and the women at the North, all talking about rights, the white men will be in a fix pretty soon. But what's all this here talking about?

What "racket" is she referring to? What is "out of kilter" in the opinion of Sojourner Truth and the other women in attendance there?

She identifies the "white men" as the enemy, in order to encourage the women to fight for their rights and overcome those who hold the power.

Second Section

That man over there says that women need to be helped into carriages, and lifted over ditches, and to have the best place everywhere. Nobody ever helps me into carriages, or over mud-puddles, or gives me any best place! And ain't I a woman? Look at me! Look at my arm! I have ploughed and planted, and gathered into barns, and no man could head me! And ain't I a woman? I could work as much and eat as much as a man - when I could get it and bear the lash as well! And ain't I a woman? I have borne thirteen children, and seen most all sold off to slavery, and when I cried out with my mother's grief, none but Jesus heard me! And ain't I a woman?

She juxtaposes the way in which white women vs. African-American women are treated in order to bring to light the hypocrisy and discrimination, so the audience will want to take action.

She uses logos (appeal to logic) when she reasons that she worked as hard as the average African-American woman of her time compared to any white American man, and this similarity enforces that women deserve the same rights as men.

She uses pathos (appeal to emotion) when she refers to having thirteen children of her own, and as a result, she connects emotionally with all other mothers in the audience as well as joins whites and blacks as she makes an appeal for equal rights.

She applies anaphora with the repetition of "And ain't I a woman?" (all in red), and this emphasizes her pride as a woman, encourages the same emotion from her audience, and makes them feel worthy of fighting for their rights, too.

Third Section

Fourth Section

Then they talk about this thing in the head; what's this they call it? [member of audience whispers, "intellect"] That's it, honey. What's that got to do with women's rights or negroes' rights? If my cup won't hold but a pint, and yours holds a quart, wouldn't you be mean not to let me have my little half measure full?

She uses ethos (appeal to ethics) when she addresses the men who hold all the power and asks if they could be fair and ethical enough to give women the same rights that men already have in America.

Fifth Section

Then that little man in black there, he says women can't have as much rights as men, 'cause Christ wasn't a woman! Where did your Christ come from? Where did your Christ come from? From God and a woman! Man had nothing to do with Him.

She continues with an allusion to the Bible here, in order to connect with the religious members of the audience, but more importantly, she reminds everyone that Christ was born from a woman. Therefore, it may stand to reason that he meant for women to have rights just as men since Christ was born from a woman.

If the first woman God ever made was strong enough to turn the world upside down all alone, these women together ought to be able to turn it back, and get it right side up again! And now they is asking to do it, the men better let them.

She makes an analogy to Eve from the Bible as an example of the first woman who used her free will and rebelled against the authority of God, so she argues men should let women set the world right and gain equal rights.

Obliged to you for hearing me, and now old Sojourner ain't got nothing more to say.

She thanks the audience for listening to her speech and finishes her speech.

Figure 2.3: Annotation of Sojourner Truth's "Ain't I a Woman?"
Sojourner Truth for "Ain't I a Woman." Copyright in the Public Domain.

ONE-SENTENCE SUMMARIES FROM EACH SECTION

<u>Possible Thesis</u>: In Sojourner Truth's speech at the Women's Convention of 1851 in Akron, Ohio, she addresses the inequalities that women and blacks faced at that time in America through her use of logos, pathos, ethos, and biblical references.

<u>Summary of 1st Section</u>: She identifies white men as the enemy and hypocrites to overcome in this struggle for equality to move the women to action against the discrimination.

<u>Summary of 2nd Section</u>: She appeals to logos when she juxtaposes her strong work ethic and labors in the fields as equal to that of men as her first opposing argument for gender equality.

<u>Summary of 3rd Section</u>: She uses pathos when she applies personal experiences as a mother of thirteen children as well as rhetorical questions and repetitions like "Ain't I a woman?" to evoke an emotional response from her audience as both women and mothers.

<u>Summary of 4th Section</u>: She appeals to ethos by reminding everyone once more that white men hold all the power, and it would be fair and ethical of them to give women the same rights.

<u>Summary of 5th Section</u>: She alludes to biblical references of Eve and the Virgin Mary in order to connect to her Christian audience on a personal level and convince others that God must have meant equal rights for both genders.

Final Revised/Typed Draft of Summary

In Sojourner Truth's speech at the Women's Convention of 1851 in Akron, Ohio, she identifies men as the enemy to overcome in this daily struggle faced by women and African Americans. She also moves these two groups to action against the discrimination when she addresses the inequalities that women and blacks faced at that time in America through her use of logos, pathos, ethos, and biblical references. Foremost, she appeals to logos when she juxtaposes her strong work ethic and labors in the fields as being on par with men as one of her opposing arguments for gender equality. Besides logos, she uses pathos when she applies personal experiences as a mother of thirteen children as well as rhetorical questions and repetitions like "Ain't I a woman?" to evoke an emotional response from her audience as both women and mothers. Along with pathos, she appeals to ethos by reminding everyone once more that the white men hold all the power, and it would be fair and ethical of them to give women the same rights. Finally, she alludes to biblical references of Eve and the Virgin Mary in order to connect to her Christian audience on a personal level and convince them that God must have meant equal rights for both genders.

The Emancipation Proclamation by the President of the United States of America, Abraham Lincoln

A Proclamation

Whereas on the 22nd day of September, A.D. 1862, a proclamation was issued by the President of the United States, containing, among other things, the following, to wit:

That on the 1st day of January, A.D. 1863, all persons held as slaves within any State or designated part of a State the people whereof shall then be in rebellion against the United States shall be then, thenceforward, and forever free; and the executive government of the United States, including the military and naval authority thereof, will recognize and maintain the freedom of such persons and will do no act or acts to repress such persons, or any of them, in any efforts they may make for their actual freedom.

That the executive will on the 1st day of January aforesaid, by proclamation, designate the States and parts of States, if any, in which the people thereof, respectively, shall then be in rebellion against the United States; and the fact that any State or the people thereof shall on that day be in good faith represented in the Congress of the United States by members chosen thereto at elections wherein a majority of the qualified voters of such States shall have participated shall, in the absence of strong countervailing testimony, be deemed conclusive evidence that such State and the people thereof are not then in rebellion against the United States.

Now, therefore, I, Abraham Lincoln, President of the United States, by virtue of the power in me vested as Commander-In-Chief of the Army and Navy of the United States in time of actual armed rebellion against the authority and government of the United States, and as a fit and necessary war measure for supressing said rebellion, do, on this 1st day of January, A.D. 1863, and in accordance with my purpose so to do, publicly proclaimed for the full period of one hundred days from the first day above mentioned, order and designate as the States and parts of States wherein the people thereof, respectively, are this day in rebellion against the United States the following, to wit:

Arkansas, Texas, Louisiana (except the parishes of St. Bernard, Palquemines, Jefferson, St. John, St. Charles, St. James, Ascension, Assumption, Terrebone, Lafourche, St. Mary, St. Martin, and Orleans, including the city of New Orleans), Mississippi, Alabama, Florida, Georgia, South Carolina, North Carolina, and Virginia (except the forty-eight counties designated as West Virginia, and also the counties of Berkeley, Accomac, Morthhampton, Elizabeth City, York, Princess Anne, and Norfolk, including the cities of Norfolk and Portsmouth), and which excepted parts are for the present left precisely as if this proclamation were not issued.

And by virtue of the power and for the purpose aforesaid, I do order and declare that all persons held as slaves within said designated States and parts of States are, and henceforward shall be, free; and that the Executive Government of the United States, including the military and naval authorities thereof, will recognize and maintain the freedom of said persons.

And I hereby enjoin upon the people so declared to be free to abstain from all violence, unless in necessary self-defence; and I recommend to them that, in all case when allowed, they labor faithfully for reasonable wages.

And I further declare and make known that such persons of suitable condition will be received into the armed service of the United States to garrison forts, positions, stations, and other places, and to man vessels of all sorts in said service.

And upon this act, sincerely believed to be an act of justice, warranted by the Constitution upon military necessity, I invoke the considerate judgment of mankind and the gracious favor of Almighty God.

Abraham Lincoln, "The Emancipation Proclamation." Copyright in the Public Domain.

Practice Activity A: Write a summary of Abraham Lincoln's "Emancipation Proclamation" by following the steps outlined in this chapter as you annotate the reading, divide the passage into sections, formulate a thesis, and write one- to two-sentence summaries of each section. Afterward, revise it for grammar, spelling, and punctuation and smooth transitions between ideas as you type up a final draft to be submitted to your instructor. Aim for approximately five to eight sentences.

SUMMARIZING NARRATIVES, PERSONAL NONFICTION ESSAYS, POETRY, AND OTHER TYPES OF LITERATURE

Similar to summarizing an essay, speech, and/or article, your summary will be approximately the length of a paragraph for literature when you focus on identifying the main character(s) and the narrator, the significance of the actions or events described in the text, the relevance of the setting and themes, and the relationship all of it has on the narrator or main character(s), especially for narratives and personal essays. In other words, you will want to include details that support your purpose. However, for poetry, you will want to consider the relevance of the tone, imagery, figurative language, prose rhythm, repetition, allusions, motifs, and meter as well.

In this synopsis, you may also need to classify the poem, such as an elegy, ekphrasis, epic, narrative, persona, and so forth. You should specify the poet and year in which the poem was written, when necessary, as you determine the implications each of these elements have on the meaning of the poem before you make some final connections and end with an insightful statement about the poet's intention and meaning of the work. See the example summary below on Edgar Allan Poe's "Eldorado" before you begin your summary on Walt Whitman's "O Captain! My Captain!" in the practice activity that follows.

For "Eldorado," you would start by reading the poem about this man's journey to this mythical city of gold that the poem's title references and then underline or highlight key words while omitting unnecessary details. Next, in your own words, write a sentence for each stanza that gathers a main point being presented on the who, what, where, when, why, and how of this poem. Finally, in two to three sentences, summarize this poem in your own words by reviewing your main points. (See the breakdown of the stanzas before the brief summary that follows the poem.)

ELDORADO (1849)

By Edgar Allan Poe

Gaily bedight,
A gallant knight,
In sunshine and in shadow,
Had journeyed long,
Singing a song,
In search of Eldorado.

But he grew old,
This knight so bold,
And o'er his heart a shadow
Fell as he found
No spot of ground
That looked like Eldorado.

And, as his strength
Failed him at length,
He met a pilgrim shadow,
"Shadow," said he,
"Where can it be,
This land of Eldorado?"

"Over the Mountains
Of the Moon,
Down the Valley of the Shadow,
Ride, boldly ride,"
The shade replied,
"If you seek for Eldorado!"

- **Stanza 1:** A brave knight (delusional like Don Quixote) searches for the legendary Eldorado by day and by night while singing.
- **Stanza 2:** He grows older while finding no Eldorado in sight, and although sad, he doesn't lose hope.
- **Stanza 3:** He grows feeble and thinks he has met a "pilgrim shadow" (might represent death) and asks where he can find Eldorado.
- **Stanza 4:** The shadow tells him that Eldorado will be reached through the Valley of Shadow, or in other words, in the afterlife: implying greater reward awaits him than the fleeting fortunes of the world. (This stanza's reference is to Valley of the Shadow of Death: Psalm 23—though I walk through the valley of the shadow of death...).

Brief Poetry Summary: In 1849, Edgar Allan Poe wrote a poem titled "Eldorado," in which he describes the journey of a brave knight who never loses hope in his search for the legendary Eldorado. After a lifelong quest, he does not quit, despite growing feeble and old. Instead, he meets a pilgrim shadow who points the way through the Valley of Shadow.

<u>Practice Activity B:</u> Write a summary of Walt Whitman's "O Captain! My Captain!" by following the steps outlined in this chapter. Keep in mind, Walt Whitman composed this elegy in honor of Abraham Lincoln, who was assassinated in 1865. Afterward, revise it for grammar, spelling, and punctuation and smooth transitions between ideas as you type up a final draft to be submitted to your instructor. Aim for approximately five sentences.

O Captain! My Captain! (1865)
By Walt Whitman

O Captain! My Captain! our fearful trip is done;
The ship has weather'd every rack, the prize we sought is won;
The port is near, the bells I hear, the people all exulting,
While follow eyes the steady keel, the vessel grim and daring:
  But O heart! heart! heart!
   O the bleeding drops of red,
    Where on the deck my Captain lies,
     Fallen cold and dead.

O Captain! My Captain! rise up and hear the bells;
Rise up—for you the flag is flung—for you the bugle trills;
For you bouquets and ribbon'd wreaths—for you the shores a-crowding;
For you they call, the swaying mass, their eager faces turning;
  Here captain! dear father!
   This arm beneath your head;
    It is some dream that on the deck,
     You've fallen cold and dead.

My Captain does not answer, his lips are pale and still;
My father does not feel my arm, he has no pulse nor will;
The ship is anchor'd safe and sound, its voyage closed and done;
From fearful trip, the victor ship, comes in with object won;
  Exult, O shores, and ring, O bells!
   But I, with mournful tread,
    Walk the deck my captain lies,
     Fallen cold and dead.

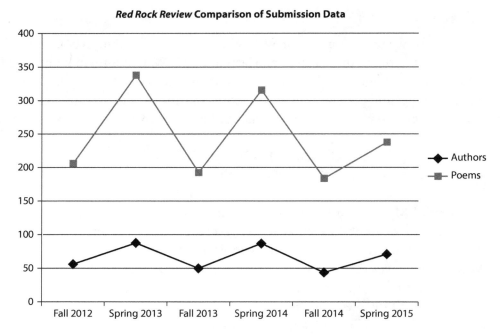

Figure 2.4 *Red Rock Review* Comparison of Submission Data

SUMMARIZING FIGURES, GRAPHS, AND TABLES

In the science or social science disciplines, you may be asked to read data from figures and tables. These visual diagrams offer quantitative results of a study as they demonstrate patterns between variables through numerical divisions, categories, and percentages. See the example summary of the information collected on submissions to the literary publication *Red Rock Review* between the fall of 2012 and spring of 2015.

Summary of Figure 2.4: According to the data collected on the *Red Rock Review*, the number of poems and authors clearly fluctuates with each submission season. For example, the number of poems and writers who submitted is substantially higher during the spring submission period, despite the fall submission period actually being longer (June to December for fall versus January to May for spring). Perhaps, even more subtly, the slight overall decline in both poets and submissions year-on-year is another striking development. This is most visible when looking at the spring submissions, where there were 338 poems in SP 2013, down to 317 in SP 2014, and an even further decline to 238 in SP 2015. Likewise, the number of submissions in the fall is still dropping, but at a visibly slower rate, with 207 in FA 2012, 193 in FA 2013, and 184 in FA 2014. As a result, one can infer the number of authors, predictably, matches this trend in poetry submissions, just on a less noticeable scale.

Practice Activity C: Write a brief summary of the data in Figure 2.5 that compares the students' response to their purpose for enrolling in a creative writing course. Consult the summary for Figure 2.4 as a model, but arrange and word your own summary differently. Aim for at least three sentences.

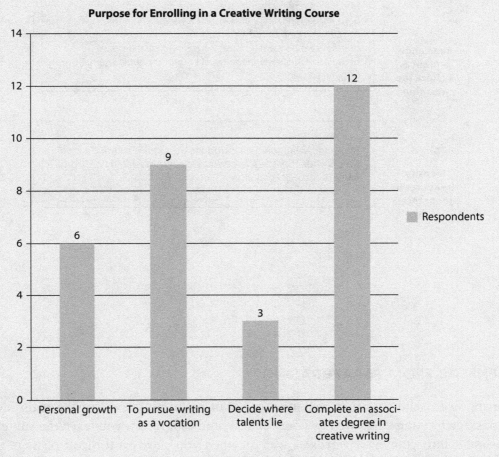

Purpose for Enrolling in a Creative Writing Course

Figure 2.5   Comparison of Data on Students' Purpose for Enrolling in a Creative Writing Course

PARAPHRASE

WHAT IS PARAPHRASE?

Paraphrase is similar to summary because you modify the passage of an author's work into your own words. However, paraphrase is different from summary in terms of being approximately the same length as the original, while summary is a shortened version of it.

Steps to Paraphrasing:

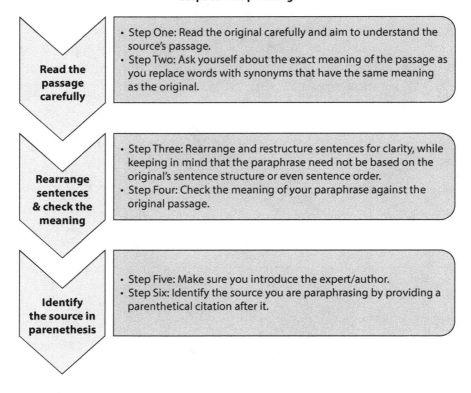

Figure 2.6

WHO BENEFITS FROM PARAPHRASING?

Paraphrasing is a useful tool that benefits you because you must explain the main ideas of a difficult passage to yourself as well as your readers, and as a result, you learn the subject when you translate it into your own words as well as when you clarify a difficult passage for your readers. It also lends you credibility as you communicate important statistics, facts, and/or numerical data, and by establishing your knowledge of the topic, you indicate to readers that you can be trusted.

WHEN SHOULD YOU USE PARAPHRASE?

You should paraphrase the details of a passage and simplify the meaning of it for yourself and your readers when the original is confusing or too difficult to understand. Furthermore, you should paraphrase when the order of the details is important but the source's wording is not necessarily memorable or striking.

HOW SHOULD YOU WRITE A PARAPHRASE?

To write a paraphrase, convert the language of another writer's passage into your own words. For instance, you read the original carefully and determine the purpose and meaning by eliminating less relevant information and extracting the main ideas to clarify the passage. You will interchange the original words with synonyms and tailor the passage to read more clearly, flow more smoothly, and demonstrate your knowledge and credibility. Here are the steps to paraphrasing.

Examples of Paraphrase:

Original Passage: In *Atlas Shrugged*, Francisco d'Anconia states, "Money is the barometer of a society's virtue" (Rand 387).

Strong Paraphrase: According to Francisco d'Anconia in *Atlas Shrugged*, currency is a measure of society's moral character (Rand 387).

Weak Paraphrase: Society's virtue is gauged by money, according to Francisco d'Anconia in *Atlas Shrugged*.

(Note: The weak paraphrase is too close to the original passage, and merely shifting or changing a few words is not enough to avoid plagiarism because it also lacks a parenthetical citation after it. The next chapter will review avoiding plagiarism and crediting your sources properly.)

<u>Practice Activity D</u>: Follow the steps and criteria for paraphrasing in the following passages.

1. "I am the lit match who burns / fast against the wind's fury / before my flame fades away" (Bailey-Kirby 1-3).
2. "Snow melt from the Himalayas is a prime source of water for Asia's major river valleys, including the Yellow, Yangtze, Meiong and Ganges. By 2070 ice-covered landmass in the Himalayas could decrease by 43 percent" (Moyer and Storrs).
3. "When we hear of extinction, most of us think of the plight of the rhino, tiger, panda, or blue whale. But these sad sagas are only small pieces of the extinction puzzle. The overall numbers are terrifying. Of the 40,168 species that the 10,000 scientists in the World Conservation Union have assessed, one in four mammals, one in eight birds, one in three amphibians, one in three conifers, and other gymnosperms are at risk of extinction" (Whitty).

4. "Richard Stevens, a cancer researcher at the University of Connecticut Health Center, has speculated that there might be a connection between breast cancer and hormone cycles disrupted by late-night light. Melatonin, primarily secreted at night, may trigger a reduction in the body's production of estrogen. But light interferes with melatonin release [recall that the hormone is secreted in response to a lack of light], allowing estrogen levels to rise. Too much estrogen is known to promote the growth of breast cancers" (Villepigue and Rivera 81).

5. "The 2010-2011 School Crime Supplement (National Center for Education Statistics and Bureau of Justice Statistics) indicates that 9% of students in grades 6-12 experienced cyberbullying. The 2013 Youth Risk Behavior Surveillance Survey finds that 15% of high school students (grades 9-12) were electronically bullied in the past year" ("Frequency of Cyberbullying").

QUOTING

WHAT IS QUOTING?

Quoting involves recording the exact language of a source. You may choose to use a direct or indirect quote in your papers. Direct quotes are always offset by quotation marks, while indirect quotes are not. And while direct quotes are the exact words of another author, indirect quotes recount what another author has stated or written in a similar fashion to summary and paraphrase. As reviewed earlier in the chapter, you briefly restate an author's work in your own words when you write a summary, while paraphrase restates a passage in your own words, except it is usually the same length as the original.

WHEN SHOULD YOU QUOTE?

You should quote an author's exact words when the language is particularly clear, striking, and concise; it contains relevant information to support your point; or it lends your discussion authority and credibility from an important expert.

In addition, you will want to quote when the language of a particular source is eloquent and powerful or when the quotation is to the point and short enough that you cannot paraphrase it without losing the meaning or confusing your readers.

You may also need to incorporate an entire table, graph, or diagram as evidence, but most importantly, you should not quote an entire lengthy paragraph if you only need one sentence or a couple of words that provide significant information (facts, statistics, numerical data, studies) to back up your stance in your thesis.

HOW DO YOU APPLY QUOTES?

You will place quotation marks around an author's words, and in most cases, you may need to include a verb for attributing a quote and follow with a comma. This will help your readers

register the shift from your voice to the source author's voice. You may want to introduce your quotations (and summaries or paraphrases) in one of the following ways:
- [Insert author or speaker] says/said (or a stronger verb from the bulleted list below)
- According to [insert author or speaker]
- In the words of [insert author or speaker]

Otherwise, it will be helpful to apply a stronger verb that implies the author's intention to be persuasive, agree or disagree, maintain a neutral stance, offer an inference, or even make a suggestion. Some helpful verbs are listed below for introducing your quotes, since you should avoid repeating the same verbs, such as *says*, *said*, *states*, or *writes*, throughout your paper.

For instance, if your objective is to be persuasive, you will want to select a strong verb like *asserts*, *argues*, *asks*, *contends*, *insists*, or *warns* in place of *says*, *said*, or *states* in your essay. In other words, try to vary the language and choose verbs that demonstrate your essay's purpose.
- Use the following verbs for an author who aims to be neutral on an issue: comments, describes, explains, illustrates, informs, notes, observes, points out, records, relates, reports, says, sees, thinks, writes.
- Use the following verbs for an author who wants to make an inference about an issue: analyzes, asks, assesses, concludes, considers, finds, instructs, predicts, proposes, reveals, shows, speculates, suggests, supposes, teaches.
- Use the following verbs for an author who disapproves of an issue: belittles, bemoans, complains, condemns, deplores, deprecates, derides, laments, warns.
- Use the following verbs for an author who wants to be persuasive about an issue: alleges, argues, claims, contends, defends, disagrees, holds, insists, maintains.
- Use the following verbs for an author who supports an issue: admits, agrees, concedes, concurs, grants.

ARE THERE SPECIAL CONDITIONS WHEN QUOTING?

You are required to use the exact words of another author when you quote directly from a source, but in some cases, you may need to alter the quotation to fit the context of your essay's text. These special situations will require a review of ellipsis, brackets, lengthy quotes (block quotations), and double quotes (single quotation marks within double quotation marks) in this next section.

For instance, you may want to omit words, phrases, sentences, or even entire paragraphs from the original work, and as a result, you may need to insert ellipsis marks (. . .) to indicate that you have removed words, phrases, and/or entire passages. To form an ellipsis, you will use three periods with a space before each period and a space after the last period (. . .) in place of the material removed from a quote. (Note: You will not have parentheses around the ellipses.)

In other words, if your quotation ends with an omission and a parenthetical citation is not used to credit an author, then you will include four periods in the ellipsis and no space before the first period or after the last one. However, if a parenthesis is used in MLA format at the end of a passage, the period will go after it.

Original Passage

"And so, my fellow Americans: ask not what your country can do for you—ask what you can do for your country. My fellow citizens of the world: ask not what America will do for you, but what together we can do for the freedom of man."

— Excerpt taken from "Ask Not What Your Country Can Do for You" speech by John F. Kennedy on January 20, 1961

Quotation with Ellipses and No Parenthetical Citation

In "Ask Not What Your Country Can Do for You," a speech by John F. Kennedy on the 20th of January, 1961, he said, "And so, . . . ask not what your country can do for you—ask what you can do for your country. My fellow citizens of the world: ask not what America will do for you, but what together we can do. . . ."

Original Passage

"Every day at eight in the morning he was brought his breakfast by Mrs. Grubach's cook—Mrs. Grubach was his landlady—but today she didn't come. That had never happened before. K. waited a little while, looked from his pillow at the old woman who lived opposite and who was watching him with an inquisitiveness quite unusual for her, and finally, both hungry and disconcerted, rang the bell."

— Excerpt taken from *The Trial* by Franz Kafka on page 1

Quotation with Ellipses and Parenthetical Citation

"Every day at eight in the morning he was brought his breakfast by Mrs. Grubach's cook—Mrs. Grubach was his landlady—but today she didn't come. That had never happened before. K. waited a little while . . . and finally, both hungry and disconcerted, rang the bell" (Kafka 1).

Furthermore, you may need to omit entire sentences from a paragraph, and if the omission starts at the end of a sentence, insert the ellipsis along with the closing punctuation of the previous sentence. In other cases, the original passage might use ellipses, and you will not be required to alter these ellipses. Instead, you will include your ellipses in square brackets [. . .] to differentiate between yours and the author's.

Original Passage

"If you want to know who won our writing contest . . . stay tuned for our upcoming announcement in the fall. We will have first place, second place, and third place winners in fiction, poetry, non-fiction, and art, and each winner will be published in the next issue of our literary and visual arts magazine."

— Excerpt taken from Yelena Bailey-Kirby's post from her personal Web site's home page: https://featuredartistnetwork.com/

Quotation with Ellipses

"If you want to know who won our writing contest . . . stay tuned for our upcoming announcement in the fall. We will have [. . .] winners in fiction, poetry, non-fiction, and art, and each winner will be published in the next issue of our literary and visual arts magazine" (Bailey-Kirby).

Practice Activity E: You will use ellipsis marks in the sentences below after you remove the underlined words. Include a parenthetical citation after each sentence with the author's last name and the page number.

1. "Journal, draw, take long walks, and meditate on what inspires you to live a more passionate life. Most importantly, surround yourself with positive people who will support you on your journey and steer clear of the negative naysayers, and as a result, you will be seizing the moment to live out the life that you were always meant to have and not wallow in regret and inertia."
   —Excerpt taken from Henrietta Palmer's blog called *Motivation Mom* on page 7

2. "It is a truth universally acknowledged, that a single man in possession of a good fortune must be in want of a wife. However little known the feelings or views of such a man may be on his first entering a neighbourhood, this truth is so well fixed in the minds of the surrounding families, that he is considered as the rightful property of someone or other of their daughters."
   —Excerpt taken from *Pride and Prejudice* by Jane Austen on page 1

3. "I am a sick man. . . . I am a spiteful man. I am an unattractive man. I believe my liver is diseased. However, I know nothing at all about my disease, and do not know for certain what ails me. I don't consult a doctor for it, and never have, though I have a respect for medicine and doctors."
   —Excerpt taken from *Notes from Underground* by Fyodor Dostoyevsky on page 1

Other instances of altering a quotation include adding square brackets for words you may need to insert within a quote to help readers understand the meaning of a quotation and avert any possible confusion about the information given in the quote.

You will provide a brief explanation within the brackets, clarify a vague pronoun within brackets, or identify a grammatical or syntactical error with brackets and add a notation of the three-letter word *sic* in italics.

However, with any kind of grammatical error, you will leave the author's passage in the original and not correct it when you do resort to using [*sic*], because this insertion will indicate to readers that the mistake was the author's, not yours. Here are the four basic rules for applying brackets when needed.

- Use brackets to clarify or add to an original quote by placing words that are being added to the original quote within those brackets.

  Original: Mr. Clark said, "The proposal was approved by the board of directors."

  Amended: Mr. Clark said, "The [advertising] proposal was approved by the board of directors."

*(Note: The vague reference the proposal is clarified with **advertising** inserted in brackets. This tells your readers exactly what you changed in the original, and it prevents confusion for your readers when they understand what proposal was accepted.)*

- Use brackets as parentheses within parentheses, especially for bibliographic references.

  Example: (For more on using apostrophes correctly, see *The Student's Handbook of Grammar and Punctuation* [2010].)

- Use brackets to demonstrate the pronunciation of a word.

  Example: She mispronounced the word *infamy* [in-fah-mi] during her speech.

- Use brackets around the Latin term [*sic*] in italics when a grammatical or syntactical error occurs, and leave the error in the original form without correcting it. (Note: *Sic* means "thus" or "such" in Latin.)

  Example: He wrote, "Harvard University is well-known for it's [*sic*] high academic standards."

Practice Activity F: You will use brackets where they are needed in the sentences below.

1. Use brackets to clarify a vague reference for the pronoun in the quote below.
   Civil War historian Jacob Maxwell writes, "He issued the Emancipation Proclamation in 1863 and promoted the passage of the Thirteenth Amendment to the United States Constitution, abolishing slavery, and as the Sixteenth President of the United States, his most famous speech was the Gettysburg Address." (Note: Clarify "He" at the beginning of the quote with "Abraham Lincoln" inserted in brackets.)

2. Use brackets as parentheses within parentheses for the bibliographic reference below.
   (For more details on using APA format, please consult the *Publication Manual of the American Psychological Association*, 2013.)

3. Use brackets for the pronunciation of a word and with *sic* in italics for a grammar or syntax error in the sentence below.
   He has trouble pronouncing hyperbole hy-per-ba-lee, but he seemed to have a harder time using words correctly when he wrote his last interoffice memo: "The office printer does not make color copies, but it's black toner allows for gray scale printouts of drafts and images."

Other special conditions include the use of lengthy passages that are more than four typed lines of prose or three lines of verse. These block quotations must be indented ten character spaces from the left margin; however, you do not insert double quotation marks around the quote like you would for shorter quotes.

You will also double-space the passage like the rest of the text in your essay, and you will use a colon to introduce the block quote, unless another type of punctuation mark would be more appropriate or none is needed based on the syntax.

In addition, you will place parenthetical citations after quoted passages, and while you place a period after the closing parentheses for shorter quotes, summaries, and paraphrased passages, block quotes are the exception to this rule. The period precedes the parenthetical citation, as the example below demonstrates. You will be asked to complete a practice activity on block quotes in the chapter on MLA format.

LENGTHY QUOTE (BLOCK QUOTATION) EXAMPLE

Many people suffer from a parasitic infection that leads to intestinal problems and difficulty losing weight, but doctors can prescribe several options:

> Treatments depend on the type of infection and can include anti-parasitic drugs, steroids, pain relievers, anti-inflammatories, anti-histomamines, and antibiotics for relief of symptoms or to treat various infections. Some herbal remedies are fig, andrographis root, garlic, wormseed, turmeric, and pumpkin seeds, among others. There are also a number of parasitic cleansing systems and herbal combination remedies available. (Shomon 113)

Furthermore, you may have an occasion when you need to quote a passage that is already itself a quote or employs quotation marks. When this happens, you will use single quotation marks inside the double quotation marks, like the examples below.

In the first example, the titles of the two poems, which would normally be surrounded by double quotation marks (like essays or article titles), have been placed in single quotation marks instead.

However, the second example shows an alternative that may occur when quoting dialogue. Hence, the dialogue will become a quote within a quote, with the original double quotation marks around the dialogue becoming single quotations marks within the double quotation marks around the entire passage.

DOUBLE QUOTE ORIGINAL EXAMPLE

Professor Yelena Bailey-Kirby posted the following reminder to her online class in Canvas: "Please do not forget to read the poems, titled 'Aubade' by Phillip Larkin and 'Gerontion' by T. S. Eliot, by Monday's class, when we will have a quiz on both poems."

SINGLE WITHIN DOUBLE QUOTATION MARKS EXAMPLE

Original: In my younger more vulnerable years my father gave me some advice that I've been turning over in my mind ever since. "When you feel like criticizing any one," he told me, "just remember that all the people in this world haven't had the advantages that you've had."
— Excerpt taken from *The Great Gatsby* by F. Scott Fitzgerald on page 1

SINGLE WITHIN DOUBLE

In *The Great Gatsby* by F. Scott Fitzgerald, the narrator says, "In my younger and more vulnerable years my father gave me some advice that I've been turning over in my mind ever since. 'Whenever you feel like criticizing any one,' he told me, 'just remember that all the people in this world haven't had the advantages that you've had'" (1).

Practice Activity G: You will use single within double quotation marks where they are needed in the sentences below. (Note: All three examples contain double quotes, and you will need to change the inner quotation marks to single ones.)

1. The music instructor announced to the class, "You will listen to the following Blues greats: "Beer Drinking Woman" by Memphis Slims and "Statesboro Blues" by Blind Willie McTell for tonight's homework."
2. Derek claims to his friend Joe, "I'm going to live my life according to Montresor's motto of "No one wounds me with Impunity" that he engraved on his family crest in "The Cask of Amontillado" by Edgar Allan Poe."
3. At the end of the story, Tyler wondered to himself, "Why did Betty Lou's father holler at him, "No boy ain't worth a dime or a billion buckets of dirty dimes to marry my daughter, so you best not show your face around here anymore" when he asked his permission to marry Betty Lou and to take care of her and both of the parents for life since becoming head foreman at the factory."

Steps for Quoting:

Short direct quotes
- Record the exact words of an author and place quotation marks around the quote, followed by a parenthetical citation with a period after it.
- Include a strong verb for attributing a quote and follow with a comma.
- Avoid quoting an entire paragraph if one sentence or a few words are more relevant to your point and provide sufficient evidence to support your thesis.

Lengthy direct quotes
- Indent block quotes of more than four typed lines of prose or three lines of verse ten characters spaces from the left margin.
- Double-space the passage and introduce the quotation with a colon unless another type of punctuation would be more appropriate.
- Place parenthetical citations after the block quote, with the period before the citation.

Special conditions
- Use ellipsis for omitting unnecessary information from a quotation.
- Apply brackets for adding information to fit grammatically and syntactically in the text of your essay.
- Insert single quotation marks within double quotation marks when you have a double quote.

Figure 2.7

CHAPTER 3
DOCUMENTING SOURCES IN MLA STYLE

Figure 3.1   Dating Game — Plagiarism Cartoon

In this chapter, you will learn about documenting sources fully and properly in MLA (Modern Language Association) format. This is a system commonly used in English and the humanities, while other disciplines apply other styles. You should ask your instructors what style they require because you may need to use APA (American Psychological Association) for education, psychology, and social sciences; Chicago/Turabian for business, history, and the fine arts; ACS (American Chemical Society) for chemistry; or even CBE (Council of Biology Editors) for biology, among several other standards, instead of the MLA method.

However, for this English course, we will only be focusing on MLA style in order to help you strengthen your credibility, demonstrate the extent of your research, and prevent any plagiarism. There are two main components to crediting your sources accurately to avoid plagiarism as well as indicating that material in your essay has been borrowed from a source. In other words, you will include an in-text parenthetical citation that refers to an author and page number within your essay (when both are given for a source) and a Works Cited list that records the full publication information at the end of your essay whenever you quote, paraphrase, and/or summarize from print and nonprint sources.

Due to the release of the eighth edition in April 2016, the MLA system for documenting sources has some new guidelines that you will need to know. This chapter will outline the principles behind applying MLA citations correctly, and by completing some practice activities, you will have a better understanding of the material reviewed in each section of this chapter.

PLAGIARISM

WHAT IS PLAGIARISM?

Plagiarism means to steal the words of another and treat them as if they were your own. It is considered unethical and an offense against the academic community when you borrow information from a source by quoting, summarizing, and/or paraphrasing from it without using proper documentation. Neglecting to credit a source might be deliberate or accidental, but either way, it still constitutes cheating when you submit a research paper or any other type of composition written in whole or in part by another as if it were your own original work. As a result, students might fail a course because instructors may assign an F for academic dishonesty as well as follow other procedures outlined by their institution's integrity policy.

HOW DO YOU AVOID PLAGIARISM?

To avoid plagiarism, you must document any material found through research by following MLA format properly and accurately. You must proofread your work carefully, consult your instructor when you have a question about citations, or even double-check your work with a writing center assistant when you have a question about acknowledging another's independent material (words unique to another author's research, theories, or ideas).

Although it is unnecessary to cite common knowledge (Andrew Jackson was the seventh president of the United States); familiar sayings, axioms, or proverbs ("Haste makes waste!"); and well-known quotations ("*The personal is political*"), any independent material (facts, opinions, statistics, studies) that you draw from another source must be documented.

If you plan to summarize, paraphrase, and/or quote (historical, statistical, or scientific facts) from any source other than your own original words and thoughts, you are required to credit your sources with author and page number in a parenthetical citation and include the full publication information in a Works Cited list at the end of your essay.

Furthermore, if you make any changes to a source's passage with omissions, you must include ellipsis marks (. . .) to indicate material was removed from the original. In addition, if you add a new phrase or substitute another term for the original language to clarify the meaning or to fit words grammatically and syntactically in the context of the sentence, you must use brackets: [ ].

PARENTHETICAL CITATIONS

What are the common patterns for placement of parenthetical citations for sources?

The in-text parenthetical citation can be arranged in one of three ways listed below. After the parenthetical documentation has acknowledged the source within the text of your essay, the reader can then consult the complete reference information for each source on the Works Cited page at the end of your essay.

- For one author, provide the author's last name and page number(s) within the parenthesis after any borrowed material, including paraphrased passages, summaries, and/or quotes, or you can identify the author's name in the text of your essay and place the page number(s) in the parenthesis. (Note: The period will follow the closing parenthesis, not precede it, for a short quote, paraphrase, or summary.)

> "The rising cost of tuition has led the majority of college students to amass a higher loan debt in 2015 upon graduation than in previous years" (Clark 43).

> According to Sarah Clark from the Senate Education Committee, "The rising cost of tuition has led the majority of college students to amass a higher loan debt in 2015 upon graduation than in previous years" (43).

- For two authors, include the last name of each source.

> (Petrov and Kowalski 168).

- For three or more authors, include the last name of the first author followed by "et al." (Latin for "and the rest") without any intervening punctuation and then give your page number(s) in the parenthesis.

> (Wright et al. 63).

- For a source by a corporate author or government agency, you can abbreviate terms that are generally abbreviated, such as Department (Dept.). In addition, when the corporate author or organization is acknowledged in the Works Cited list by the names of administrative units separated by commas, cite all the names with the page number(s) in the parenthesis. Otherwise, you may introduce the names in the text and then only include page numbers in the parenthesis.

> (United States, Dept. of Labor 123).

Works Cited

United States, Department of Labor. *The Energy Employees Occupational Illness Compensation Program.* Government Printing Office, 2001.

A report by the Bureau of Firearms explains their responsibility for identifying an individual's ineligibility to acquire or possess firearms and other weapons (12).

- For an anonymous work or source with no author, provide either the whole title of the work in the text or use a shortened version of the title in the parenthesis with the page number(s). In other words, you can abbreviate the title to one word or the first couple of words in the parenthetical citation. (Note: Insert quotation marks around the titles of articles and italicize the titles of books.)

    Marginalization of Women notes females face more violence within public and private spaces and are doubly oppressed by norms, culture and customs in a male-dominated world (29).

    OR

    (*Marginalization* 29).

- For a source with no page numbers, which is often the case with Web pages, include the section or paragraph number in your parenthetical citation if it is available. However, omit the numbers if no such reference marks have been used in the source. (Note: Label it par. or pars. for paragraphs; ch. or chs. for chapters; and sec. or secs. for sections.)

    Foster argues that "O'Reilly appropriated government funds illegally before he sought asylum abroad" (par. 18).

    "Determinism is the philosophical belief that every event, decision, or human action is the inevitable and necessary outcome of a precursory state of affairs" (Smith).

- For works in verse like plays and poems, provide line numbers from the margins; in other words, do not include page numbers, but cite by division (act, scene, canto, book, part) and line, separating the numbers with periods. However, if you are citing only line numbers for a poem, for instance, refer to the word line or lines in your first citation, and then, once you have established that the numbers designate lines, you can simply give the numbers alone in the rest of your essay.

    One of William Shakespeare's characters, named Polonius, tells Laertes, "This above all: to thine own self be true" (Ham. 1:3. 564).

    Dylan Thomas asserts, "Old age should burn and rave at close of day" (line 2).

When you quote part or all of a line of verse without a need for special emphasis, place quotation marks around it like you would for a line of prose and insert a forward slash with a space on each side (/) to show your reader where the line breaks should fall for two or three lines that you cite. However, to indicate where a stanza break occurs in the quotation, use two forward slashes (//).

> In "Bright Star," John Keats wrote, "Still, still to hear her tender-taken breath, / And so live ever—or else swoon to death" (lines 13-14).

> In "Parsley" by Rita Dove, the speaker explains, "The cane appears // in our dreams" (lines 15-16).

Verse quotations of more than three lines should be set off from your text in a block quote by indenting it half an inch from the left margin, unless the quoted verse entails unusual spacing, like the poem "Grasshopper" by E. E. Cummings that follows as an example. Do not place quotation marks around the verse that are not already included in the original lines.

According to William Butler Yeats in "Easter, 1916," "living" things and people who are hindered by the "stream" of change, as characterized in the reference to the transfer of seasons, and who fill their "Hearts with one purpose alone" will become as hard, stubborn, and static as a stone:

> Hearts with one purpose alone
> Through summer and winter seem
> Enchanted to a stone
> To trouble the living stream. (lines 41-44)

In "Grasshopper," E. E. Cummings demonstrates the vitality of a grasshopper's jumping through his use of spatial configuration, line breaks, and sequential motion of words and letters to correspond to hops and leaps from line to line:

> r-p-o-p-h-e-s-s-a-g-r
>   who
> a)s w(e loo)k
> upnowgath
>   PPEGORHRASS
>   erring. (1-5)

By unscrambling the lines, letters, and words from their erratic arrangement, one deduces that he wrote: the grasshopper who as we look up now gathering.

- For citing scripture, identify by divisions of the work—for the Bible or other sacred books. In other words, provide the abbreviated name of the book, chapter, and verse. Note: Use a period between the chapter and verse numbers instead of a page number in the parenthesis. When you borrow from a particular work of scripture, like the Bible, Koran, or Talmud, you should also refer in the text or in a parenthetical citation to the component (e.g., title of the edition, an editor's name, or a translator's name) that begins the entry in the Works Cited list.

In finding salvation, forgiveness is the key ingredient emphasized in several Bible passages of the *New International Version*: "For if you forgive other people when they sin against you, your heavenly Father will also forgive you" (Matt. 6.14), and "In him we have redemption through his blood, the forgiveness of sins, in accordance with the riches of God's grace" (Ephes. 1.7).

- For citing a quote that is referenced in another source, denote the source you actually consulted in your parenthetical citation and in your Works Cited. Hence, if only an indirect source is available, use the abbreviation qtd. in to show that the information was quoted in another source. (Note: You may want to explain the relation between the original and secondhand sources in a note.)

    Colleen Marlow confessed her political affiliation stands "between moderate and democratic-socialist" (qtd. in Burrows 2: 390).

- For a lengthy passage (block quotation) that extends to more than four typed lines of prose or three lines of poetry, as mentioned earlier, indent the entire passage (half an inch from the left margin). However, do not indent the first line more than the rest of the passage, and do not use double quotation marks around the passage. Double-space the passage like the text in your essay, and use a colon to introduce the block quotation (unless another type of punctuation mark would be more appropriate or none at all). Finally, remember for lengthy quotations to place punctuation before the parenthetical citation, not after it like for shorter quotations, paraphrased passages, or summaries.

Push-ups can help strengthen your back, shoulders, and upper arms and can easily

be performed anywhere with the following steps:

Lie face down and place your hands on the floor with palms facing

downward and wider than your shoulders. You can choose to do an easier

push-up if you are a beginner with knees on the floor or, if you are more

advanced, position your feet/toes on the floor for a full push-up. Aim to

hold your back and legs straight as you exhale and push your body away

from the floor with your arms. Then inhale while you lower your body

toward the ground except avoid touching the ground. Repeat this routine

as often as you can, and you will improve your form each day. (Hogan 99)

- For two or more sources by the same author, the most complete citation includes the author's last name, followed by a comma and the title of the work. You may need to shorten the title, and then provide the page number in the parenthesis. However, it would be easiest on you to place the author's name in the text or both the author's name and title of the work in the text, and then you only need to refer to the page number(s) in the parenthesis.

> Some personal revelations come from the same woman who originally wrote: "The outsider reigns terror on the common man's ignorance until they reach enlightenment and can reach out to the outside with courage and faith" (Kurtz, *Insiders and Outsiders* 47), but in later years, she also reveals her growth and development: "It was not very long before I was taught proper etiquette and all the social graces to be ready for my first high society ball" (Kurtz, *American Debutante* 92).

> OR

> Some personal revelations come from Michelle Kurtz, who originally wrote: "The outsider reigns terror on the common man's ignorance until they reach enlightenment and can reach out to the outside with courage and faith" (*Insiders and Outsiders* 47), but in later years, she also reveals her growth and development: "It was not very long before I was taught proper etiquette and all the social graces to be ready for my first high society ball" (*American Debutante* 92).

> OR

> According to Michelle Kurtz in *Insiders and Outsiders*, "The outsider reigns terror on the common man's ignorance until they reach enlightenment and can reach out to the outside with courage and faith" (47); in later years, she also reveals her growth and development in *American Debutante*: "It was not very long before I was taught proper etiquette and all the social graces to be ready for my first high society ball" (92).

- For works by more than one author who share the same last name (e.g., Francis Kidwell, who wrote the "The Dangers of Nuclear Energy," and Terence Kidwell, who wrote the article "Preventing Another Chernobyl Disaster"), avoid ambiguity in the citation by adding the authors' first initial before their last name in the parenthetical citation, along with the page number. However, if the first name's initial is also shared, include the full first name.

> Authorities reference two major nuclear disasters to warn governments against the dangers of nuclear energy and the need for countermeasures to be in place, in order to prevent future accidents: "Natural disasters like tsunami waves struck the Fukushima Daiichi nuclear energy facility's reactors and disabled their system needed to cool the nuclear fuel, and it has resulted in irreversible damage on the environment, especially in the Pacific Ocean" (F. Kidwell 9), and while "Chernobyl

Continued

occurred due to a faulty reactor design and human error, the radiation has increased cases of thyroid cancer, cataracts, leukemia, and birth defects" (T. Kidwell 9).

Practice Activity A: Apply MLA format for parenthetical in-text citations at the end of each quote, summarized passage, and/or paraphrased sentence below.

1. Provide a parenthetical citation for an anonymous source titled "Revisiting Sonnet Forms," which was published in *Poetry Studies Encyclopedia* in 1999. Note, anonymous means there is no author for the paraphrased passage that appears on page 6.

    Although both the Spenserian and Shakespearean sonnets follow iambic pentameter, the former involves "abab, bcbc, cdcd ee" for the rhyme scheme, while the latter holds to the "abab, cdcd, efef, gg" pattern.

2. Provide a parenthetical citation for a block quote from a source titled *Marriage Rules*, which was published by Tyndale in 2011. Note, there is only one author, named Jacob Nazarene, and the passage appears on page 189.

    The rules of a successful marriage are clearly outlined for newlyweds and seasoned couples in *Marriage Rules*:

    > First, you must marry the right person: one whom you love and one who loves you. Second, give and take is a necessity. Let love cover the disagreements which will come in any marriage. Three, never carry into tomorrow the petty troubles of today. Forgive at the end of the day, and then forget. Four, do not discuss your disagreements and personal problems with others. You will soon forget these quarrels, but others will remember them forever. Five, try to live within your financial means. Do not try to keep up with other couples; keep within your income. And be sure to set aside something for a rainy day.

3. Provide a parenthetical citation for a source, titled *A Parent's Guide to Children with ADHD*, which was published by Allyn in 1990. Note, there are more than three authors—Nora Stossel, Cindy Lombard, Farhana Kumar, and Jennifer Keller—to cite for the passage that appears on page 25. (Hint: You will use et al.)

    "Reduce your children's symptoms of hyperactivity, impulsivity, and inattentiveness by removing junk food from their diets and encouraging daily physical activity because it will improve their concentration and reduce their anxiety."

THE BASICS OF A WORKS CITED LIST AND THE CORE ELEMENTS OF AN ENTRY

The in-text parenthetical citations grant your reader only partial information, so you must include the complete reference details in a list, titled "Works Cited," at the end of your essay. If the last page of your essay's text is 8, then this list should start on page 9. Your last name and the page number will appear in the upper right-hand corner, half an inch from the top.

Next, you will type "Works Cited" without the double quotations marks around it and center it, one inch from the top. Then, arrange the list of sources alphabetically by author's last name, but if you have an anonymous work, list it under the first word of the title or under the second word if the first word is *A*, *An*, *The*, or comparable foreign terms like *El* in Spanish or *Le* and *La* in French. In addition, you should start each entry flush with the left margin, but if an entry runs to more than one line, indent five spaces for each succeeding line of the entry and double-space each entry as well as between entries.

Moreover, if you are using two or more sources by the same author, the work whose title comes earlier in the alphabet should be listed before the work whose title comes later in the alphabet. There will be three hyphens in place of the author's name for the second and subsequent entries. Specific examples follow for each type of source in order to show you the order of the elements to cite.

Abide by the guidelines outlined in this chapter for the various types of sources to help you understand the basic patterns for organizing the information accurately. Note that some of the changes from the seventh edition to the eighth edition include "Containers," along with using the phrase "Accessed on" instead of listing the date or abbreviations like "n.d." Furthermore, medium of publication will no longer be identified when documenting your sources; commas will be used in place of periods between publisher, publication date, and pagination; and DOIs (digital object identifiers) will be cited instead of URLs when they are available.

Here is the model to use with the core elements and correct punctuation when generating a citation in MLA format as it should appear in your Works Cited:

CORE ELEMENTS	MLA CITATION GENERATOR
Author.	_____.
Title of source.	_____.
Title of container,	_____,
Other contributors,	_____,
Versions,	_____,
Number,	_____,
Publisher,	_____,
Publication date,	_____,
Location.	_____.

An element listed above may be excluded from an entry if it is not relevant to the work being documented, and there will be some variations from one medium to another since there could be a second "Container" with additional information to record. Otherwise, each part listed above should follow the punctuation mark given, except for the final component, which will end with a period. You may want to consult the *MLA Handbook* (8th ed.) and apply the practice template version when documenting other print and nonprint sources that have more extensive information to document. (See the practice template version that follows, since it has two sets of "Containers" that you may need to apply for Web sources and so forth.)

MLA (8th ED.) PRACTICE TEMPLATE	
1) Author.	
2) Title of source.	
CONTAINER 1	
3) Title of container,	
4) Other contributors,	
5) Version,	
6) Number,	
7) Publisher,	
8) Publication date,	
9) Location.	
CONTAINER 2	
3) Title of container,	
4) Other contributors,	
5) Version,	
6) Number,	
7) Publisher,	
8) Publication date,	
9) Location.	

WHAT FORM IS USED FOR BOOKS?

Books must include the primary information of author, title, publisher, and publication date. Although specific examples follow to help you, remember to italicize the titles of sources that are self-contained and independent, like a book or novella, and the titles of containers, such as anthologies or Web sites. On the other hand, you should enclose titles within quotation marks for titles of shorter sources (e.g., poems, short stories, journal articles, etc.) that are contained in a larger body of work.

Another important factor is applying capitalization of your titles correctly. Capitalize the following parts of speech in your titles, as the bulleted list below illustrates with a few examples to help you understand:
- Nouns: person (mother), place (city), or thing (road)—*The Road to Motherhood*
- Pronouns: our, my, your, etc.—*Our Father's War*
- Verbs: walks, run, dances, etc.—*Dances with Wolves*
- Adjectives: beautiful, tiny, large, etc.—*The Beautiful American*
- Adverbs: loudly, softly, gently, etc.—*Death Sung Softly*
- Subordinating conjunctions: although, because, if, etc.—*Two If by Sea*

The following parts of speech are not capitalized when they come in the middle of a title, so avoid capitalizing the following:
- Articles: a, an, the—*When the Emperor Was Divine*
- Prepositions: against, between, in, etc.—*A Goddess in the Stones: Travels in India*
- Coordinating conjunctions: FANBOYS (for, and, nor, but, or, yet, so)—*Lily and Miss Liberty*

- The *to* in infinitives—*How to Win Friends and Influence People*

Now, the basic format for a book with some variations and omissions includes the following example, along with many other types of sources that will show you the core elements to use for your citations:

Last Name, First Name. *Title of Book*. Publisher, Publication Date.

Author	Title	Publisher	Publication Date
Miller, Sullivan.	*The Assassin's Code.*	Random House,	1995.

A book by a single author

Weaver, Barry. *Nikola Tesla: The Father of Invention*. Norton, 2012.

A book by two authors

Sands, Jeffrey, and Maureen Zane. *The American Revolution*. Simon and Schuster, 2003.

A book with more than three authors

Thomson, Derek, et al. *American Gentrification*. Harvard UP, 1998.

(Note: You should record the name of the first person listed on the title page and add the Latin "et al.," meaning "and the rest," after the inverted name.)

Two or more books by the same author

Kramer, Cecilia. *Advertising Appeals in the Twenty-First Century*. HarperCollins, 2008.

--- *Marketing Methods in the Media*. HarperCollins, 2011.

(Note: You should provide the author's full name with the first entry, but for the second and any additional works, open with three hyphens that stand for the exact same name(s) as the previous entry and then follow with a period and the title. Remember to alphabetize the entries by the books' titles.)

A book written under a pseudonym

Stendhal. *The Charterhouse of Parma*. Translated by Richard Howard, Modern Library, 1999.

An anonymous book

The Complete Reference Guide to Serial Killers. Harcourt, 1993.

An edited book

Johnson, Olivia S., and Winston McGuire, editors. *Mythology and Ancient Cultures: Original Texts and Sources*. Viking-Penguin, 1987.

A translation

Cooper, Helen, and Bradley Truman, translators. *The Rhetoric and Poetics of Aristotle.* By Aristotle, Farrar, 1993.

A book in two or more volumes

Findlay, Janet. *The History of the Women's Movement.* Vol. 3, Harvard UP, 1981.

A book in its second or subsequent edition

Greene, Benjamin, editor. *Political Correctness in the Media.* 5th ed. Harcourt, 2013.

Republished book (reprint of an earlier work)

Emory, Joseph. *The Beast of Burden.* 1950. Routledge, 1988.

(Note: Record the original date of publication before the publication date for books that have been reprinted due to popularity, even if they are not being republished as a new and revised edition and no changes or updates are being made.)

A book with two or more publishers

Hamilton, James, and William Jackson. *The Rise and Fall of the Third Reich.* Knopf/ Bantam, 1997.

(Note: If two or more organizations are named in the source as responsible for producing or publishing the source, then cite both of them by separating their names with a forward slash: /.)

A corporate (or governmental author)

American Medical Association. *American Medical Association Family Medical Guide.* Wiley, 2004.

(Note: A corporate or governmental author may consist of an agency, committee, commission, or other group such as the United Nations or the Economic Commission of Africa that does not refer to individual members on the title page. Hence, you will need to record the names of the corporate authors where you would normally list the names of individual authors at the beginning of your entry.)

A government publication

United States, Government Accountability Office. *Climate Change: Observations on EPA's April 1999 Climate Change Report.* Government Printing Office, 1999.

The Bible

> The Bible. Authorized King James Version, Oxford UP, 1998.

> The Holy Bible. New International Version, Zondervan, 2011.

A preface, introduction, foreword, or afterword

> Esposito, Denise. Preface. *Women in the Renaissance: Motherhood to Monarchy,* translated by Stephanie Heinzman. Ballatine, 1977, pp. vi-x.

An article in a reference book (e.g., dictionaries, encyclopedias, etc.)

> "Irony." *The New American Webster Handy College Dictionary.* 1981.

(Note: Cite this entry like you would any other work in a collection, except omit the publisher information; if organized alphabetically, you do not need to identify the volume or page number for this reference source.)

One or more volumes in a multivolume work

> Dumas, Alexander. *The Three Musketeers.* Translated by Elsa Davenport, vol. 2, Prentice, 2002.

(Note: If you only need to cite one volume of a multivolume work, identify the volume number after the book's title, or even after the editor or translator, depending on the source. Otherwise, document the book without referencing the other volumes like an independent publication when the volume has its own title, or include the total number of volumes if you are citing more than one volume from a multivolume work.)

A work in an anthology or collection

> Gordon, Neal. "Jim Crow Laws: Mandated Racial Segregation." *The Anthology of the Civil Rights Movement,* edited by James Mulligan and Deborah Tate. Wadsworth, 1976, pp. 149-57.

(Note: When you cite a work in an anthology, provide the inclusive page numbers used.)

Practice Activity B: Cite the following book sources as they would appear on a Works Cited page by using the information provided below. Remember to apply correct punctuation and formatting.

1. For a book by one author, list it in the correct order by following MLA format.

   Author: Claudette Harley
   Book Title: *The Songbird's House*
   Publisher: MacMurray
   Date of Publication: 1999

2. For an edited book, list it in the correct order by following MLA format.

   Editor: Philip Smith
   Book Title: *100 Best-Loved Poems*
   Publisher: Dover
   Date of Publication: 1995

3. For a source with more than three authors, list it in the correct order by following MLA format and using the phrase et al. (Latin for "and others") in place of the subsequent authors' names. (Note that there is a period after "al" in "et al." Also, there is never a period after the "et" in "et al.")

   Authors: Ann Mitts, John Wallace, Chloe Stubbs, and Geoffrey Reiner
   Book Title: *Negotiation Strategies: Winning without Concession*
   Publisher: Morrow
   Date of Publication: 2004

What form is used for periodicals: articles in journals, newspapers, and magazines accessed in print?

Articles from various periodicals, such as magazines, newspapers, and scholarly journals, that appear in print require three main elements: the author of the article, the title of the article with double quotation marks around it, and information about/name of the magazine, newspaper, or journal in italics. In addition, MLA employs the label "Container" in reference to any print or digital venue like a print journal or Web site that features an article or essay. When citing a specific date for a monthly publication, abbreviate the months that are longer than four letters:

Jan.	Apr.	Oct.
Feb.	Aug.	Nov.
Mar.	Sept.	Dec.

Other abbreviations to keep in mind when citing periodicals include the following: no. for number; p. or pp. for page/pages; vol. for volume, ed. for edition; or et al. ("and others" when referring to three or more authors) as mentioned earlier in the chapter. Review the list of abbreviations discussed earlier in this chapter to refresh your memory. Besides remembering to use these abbreviations, you will need to list a DOI (digital object identifier), URL (the address of a Web page), or permalink (a static hyperlink to a specific Web page or entry in a blog) when applicable.

Here is the basic format for a periodical, with some variations or omissions of core elements, depending on anonymous articles, absence of translators, or other factors, as the examples in this section will demonstrate:

Author. Title. Title of container (self-contained if book), Other contributors (translators or editors), Version (edition), Number (vol. and/or no.), Publisher, Publication Date, Location (pp.). 2nd container's title, Other contributors, Version, Number, Publisher, Publication date, Location.

Author.	Title.	Publisher,	Publication Date (Day Month Year),	Pages
Pratt, Bradley.	"How to Wear Scarves with a Suit."	GQ,	17 Dec. 2013,	pp. 9–13.

OR

Author.	Title.	Number (vol. and/or no.),	Publisher,	Publication Date,	Pages
Gibbs, Melanie.	"Our Welfare System."	vol. 12, no. 5,	*Journal of Western Economics,*	2013,	pp. 63–79.

OR

Author.	Title.	Publisher,	Publication Date,	Location.
Hernandez, Carlos.	"Middle Class and Hungry in Venezuela."	*New York Times,*	10 Aug. 2016,	www.nytimes.com/2016/08/10/opinion/middle-class-and-hungry-in-venezuela.html?action=click&pgtype=Homepage&clickSource=story-heading&module=opinion-c-col-right-region&region=opinion-c-col-right-region&WT.nav=opinion-c-col-right-region.

Cite the core elements that are available to you as the three different entries for the sources above demonstrate; however, you will most likely omit other information that is not available or applicable to your periodical.

Article in a monthly magazine

Foster, Natalie. "Stonehenge Rituals and the Winter Solstice." *Anthropology Monthly,* Nov. 2014, pp. 70–74.

(Note: Cite the article's author, placing quotations marks around the title of the article, and italicize the periodical title. Then, follow with the date of publication by abbreviating the month and end with the page range.)

Article in a weekly magazine

Brown, Kevin. "GMO's: What You Need to Know." *Nutrition Today*, 18 Feb. 2015, pp. 76–83.

An anonymous article

"Hybrid Cars." *Auto Consumer*, 3 Aug. 2011, pp. 17–24.

An article from a newspaper

Emerson, Margaret. "The Traditional Julian Calendar Still under Dispute in the West." *Eastern Orthodoxy News*, 7 March 2013, p. 29.

(Note: Cite a newspaper article just as you would a magazine article, but the pagination in a newspaper will be different. For instance, if there is more than one edition available for a date, depending on an early or late edition of a newspaper, then list the edition after the article title.)

Rudd, Patrick. "New IVCC Students Must Attend Convocation." *The Main Street Courier* [Oglesby, IL], 7 Aug. 2009, p. 21.

(Note: Cite the city name in brackets after the title of the newspaper if it is a less well-known or a local publication.)

An article from a newspaper with lettered sections

Redford, Carl. "How to Make Money in Stocks." *Investor's Business Daily*, 18 Oct. 2010, B1+.

(Note: Cite only the first page number or section letter before the page number, with a plus sign and no intervening spacing if a work in a periodical is not printed on consecutive pages.)

An editorial and letter to the editor

"Student Loan Debt Crisis." Editorial. *Springfield Sun*, western edition, 20 Sept. 2012, p. A16.

Meechum, Arlene. Letter. *Northwest Journalism Review*, Dec. 2014/Jan. 2015, p. 9.

(Note: Include the designators "Editorial" and "Letter" to distinguish the kind of work it is from other articles in a periodical.)

An anonymous article

"Fish Oil Tied to Better Brain Function." *Men's Health Daily*, 22 June 2001, p. 37.

(Note: Cite the title of the article when it is an anonymous article and the remaining core elements that you would use for any other type of periodical.)

A review

Driscoll, Hillary T. "The Thin Line between Love and Hate." Review of *The Unmasked Woman*, directed by Francois Goddard. *New York Times*, 5 May 2003, p. E8.

(Note: Record the author's name, title of the review if it is available, the phrase "Review of" and then the title of the work in italics for books, plays, and films or in quotation marks for articles, poems, and short stories. Afterward, list the performance and/or remaining publication information.)

Article in a scholarly journal

D'Angelo, Gerome. "Dialects and Idioms." *Journal of Linguistic Studies*, vol. 36, no. 2, 2007, pp. 198–214.

(Note: Cite the author and title of the article as you normally would for other periodicals, and since a scholarly journal is considered a container like a collection of shorts stories or poems, a television series, a Web site, or any larger body of work, you must place the title of the journal in italics afterward. Then, you should identify the volume number ("vol.") and issue number ("no.") whenever possible, separating them with commas and adding the year and page numbers at the end.)

An article in a special issue of a scholarly journal

Meadows, Timothy. "The Last Prayer before the Fall of Man." *Literature and Religion*, special issue of *Journal of Modern Literary Studies*, vol. 3, no. 2, 1998, pp. 14–23.

(Note: Place the title of an article that was published in a special issue of a journal in quotation marks, followed by a period. Then cite the name of the special issue in italics, followed by a comma. Also include the descriptor "special issue of" along with the name of the journal and any remaining information vital for a citation in a scholarly journal.)

Practice Activity C: Cite the following periodical sources as they would appear on a Works Cited page in MLA format by using the information provided below. Remember to apply correct punctuation and formatting.

1. Apply the correct MLA format for an article in a journal.

   Author's Name: Cody Bowers and Shane Grey
   Title of Article/Essay: "U.S. Affairs in the EU"
   Title of Periodical: *Journal of Western Politics*
   Volume: 2 & Issue Number: 2
   Date of Publication: 2014

2. Apply the correct MLA format for an article in a monthly magazine.

   Author's Name: Terence Hayes
   Title of Article/Essay: "Gourmet on a Budget"
   Title of Periodical: *Haute Cuisine Magazine*
   Date of Publication: April 2010
   Page Range: 89-96

3. Apply the correct MLA format for an anonymous article in a weekly magazine.

   Title of Article/Essay: "The Health Benefits of Yoga"
   Title of Periodical: *Women's Health Weekly*
   Date of Publication: May 18, 2007
   Page Range: 68–72

What form is used for electronic and online database sources?

For online sources, you may require more information than for a printed source. To maintain accurate information for the purpose of proper documentation and future reference, you are encouraged to apply the bookmark feature in your Web browser to easily find the electronic texts again. You also may want to print out or save copies of documents that you find through research by creating a file that stores these items on your computer. Otherwise, since the purpose of citations is for readers to be able to locate the sources you have used, you should aim to include any of the items listed below that are relevant and available.

In the eighth edition, you will need to include the URL/electronic address for most Web sources, but you should simply include the www. address and omit all https:// when citing URLs in MLA format. Nonetheless, if you have access to the permalink, which is the stable and shortened version of a URL, you should cite that instead of the URL, while it is preferable to cite the DOI (digital object identifier, used for many scholarly articles in databases) instead of the URL.

However, since most Web addresses are not static and may change over time or documents can be found in multiple databases on the Web, MLA also advises citing containers, such as

YouTube, Hulu, JSTOR, Spotify, or Netflix. Besides these guidelines for Web sources, there are abbreviations that should be applied to your citations if there are no page numbers, such as par. or pars. to refer to paragraph numbers for an electronic source instead of p. or pp. typically used for page numbers in books or periodicals.

MLA also recommends the use of the phrase "Accessed on" to indicate the date on which you accessed the Web page when no copyright date was listed on a Web site, but this is optional and not necessary in most cases. More customary requirements that you need to include are as follows: the author and/or editor names when they are available, not anonymous; the article name in quotation marks; title of the Web site, project, or book in italics; versions, editions (ed.), revisions, posting dates, volumes (vol.), and/or issue numbers (no.) if available; and publisher information (publisher's name and publication date).

Then, you may or may not have page numbers (p. or pp.) or paragraph numbers (par. or pars.) to cite. As stated earlier, if there is no copyright date, you may want to add the date you accessed ("Accessed on") the source if it is pertinent and applicable, even though it is not required. Finally, you should identify the permalink, DOI, or URL without the https:// and credit containers after the common features for documenting in MLA format.

Here is the basic format for a Web source with some variations or omissions of core elements, depending on the available information online, as the examples in this section will demonstrate:

Author. Title. Title of container (self-contained if book), Other contributors (translators or editors), Version (edition), Number (vol. and/or no.), Publisher, Publication Date, Location (pages, paragraphs and/or URL, DOI or permalink). 2nd container's title, Other contributors, Version, Number, Publisher, Publication date, Location, Date of Access (if relevant).

Author.	Title of Online Source/ Article.	Title of the 1st Container,	Number (vol. &/or no.),	Publication Date.	Title of 2nd Container,	DOI, URL, or Permalink.
Stokes, W. S.	"Animals and the 3Rs in Toxicology Research and Testing."	*Human and Experimental Toxicology,*	vol. 34, no. 12,	2015.	*ProQuest,*	doi.org.ezproxy.li brary.csn.edu/10.1177/ 0960327115598410.

An article in a Web magazine

Schoenfeld, Brad. "The Post Workout Anabolic Window." *Muscular Development,* 3 June 2016, musculardevelopment.com/articles/nutrition/15240-the-post-work out-anabolic-window.html#.V6zt7I-cFjo. Accessed on 5 June 2016.

Citing an entire website

MayoClinic. Mayo Foundation for Medical Education and Research, 1998, www.mayoclinic.org/. Accessed on 7 May 2014.

(Note: Begin with the editor, author, or compiler's name if it is available, and then provide the name of the site; version number; name of institution/organization associated with the site, such as a sponsor or publisher; the date on which the resources were created if it is available; the URL, DOI, or permalink in full without the http://; and finally the date of access if applicable.)

A published article from an online database (or other electronic subscription service)

Dolgin, Elie. "Animal Testing Alternatives Come Alive in US." *Nature Medicine*, vol. 16, no. 12, 2010. *ProQuest*, doi.org.ezproxy.library.csn.edu/10.1038/nm1210-1348.

OR

Schick, Joseph S. "The Origin of 'The Cask of Amontillado.'" *American Literature*, vol. 6, no. 1, 1934, pp. 18–21. *JSTOR*, www.jstor.org/stable/2919684.

(Note: Provide a citation for articles from an online database, such as LexisNexis, ProQuest, JSTOR, or ScienceDirect, and other subscription services as containers. Then, identify the title of the database in italics before providing the DOI or URL and list the date of access if you wish, since it is optional and not required.)

An article from an online reference source (i.e., online encyclopedia or dictionary)

Weber, Jennifer L. "American Civil War." *Encyclopædia Britannica Online*. Encyclopedia Britannica Inc., 11 May 2016, www.britannica.com/event/American-Civil-War. Accessed on 29 Sept. 2016.

(Note: Follow the standard documentation format for a Web entry for an online article.)

An online news source

Friedman, Terry. "U.S. Violent Crime Up for First Time in Years." *CNN*. Turner Broadcasting System, Inc., 17 October 2012, cnn.com/2012/10/17/us/violent-crime/index.html. Accessed on 23 July 2013.

(Note: Follow the standard documentation form for a Web entry, with author's or creator's last name and then first name, the title of the piece in quotation marks, the name of the Web site in italics, the Web site publisher, date of the publication, the URL, and date of access if applicable.)

A page on a Web site

"Lactose Intolerance—Topic Overview." *WebMD*, 21 July 2014, www.webmd.com/digestive-disorders/tc/lactose-intolerance-topic-overview.

Zoe, Lance. "How to Be a Bartender at Your Next Party." *eHow*, www.ehow.com/ how_4540241_bartend-party.html. Accessed on 8 Aug. 2016.

(Note: Provide the author or an alias if it is known for an individual page on a Web site, or if it is anonymous, begin with the title on the page and publication date. Also, when the publisher and Web site's name are the same, only cite it once, then the URL, and finally, the date of access when applicable.)

An image (painting, sculpture, or photography) on the Web

Monet, Claude. *Water Lilies*. 1902, oil on canvas, Art Institute of Chicago. *Artchive*, www.artchive.com/artchive/M/monet/waterlil.jpg.html. Accessed on 19 June 2016.

(Note: Cite the artist's name, the work of art in italics, the date of creation, the medium of the composition if applicable, the institution and city where the work is housed—or omit the name of the city if it is in the name of the institution, like Art Institute of Chicago. Finally, provide the name of the Web site in italics and the date of access if applicable.)

A listserv, discussion group, or blog posting

Lamb, Evelyn. "Why You Should Care about High-Dimensional Sphere Packing." *Roots of Unity*, Scientific American Blogs, 29 July 2016, blogs.scientificamerican.com/ roots-of-unity/why-you-should-care-about-high-dimensional-sphere-packing/.

(Note: Cite the author of the work, the title of the posting in quotation marks, the Web site name in italics, the publisher, and the posting date along with the date of access if you wish, since it is optional. Include screen names as author names if they are available when the author name is unknown. Otherwise, put the author's name in brackets when both names are known.)

An e-mail (including e-mail interviews)

Hamilton, Mary. "Re: MLA Workshop." Received by Zack C. Moore, 11 Dec. 2008.

(Note: Refer to the subject as the title when you document an e-mail message. The subject is enclosed in quotation marks and its capitalization standardized, while the date given should refer to the date on which the e-mail was sent.)

A tweet

@Submittable. "Deadline Aug 31st: The Barthelme Prize for Short Prose judged by Jim Shepard." *Twitter*, 11 Aug. 2016, 3:52 p.m., twitter.com/submittable/ status/763840542677561347.

(Note: Cite the user's Twitter handle in place of an author's name, and then put the tweet in quotations mark. You should also identify the date and time of the posting, referring to the

reader's time zone, separating the date and time with a comma, and ending the citation with a period. However, if you see it relevant, add the date accessed as well.)

YouTube video (audio or video from a Web site)

"Bill Burr - You People Are All the Same 2012." *YouTube*, uploaded by Bill Burr, 29 May

2016, www.youtube.com/watch?v=N_qWBRq-z1w.

(Note: If the author's name is identical to the uploader of the video or audio source, only cite the author once. However, if it deviates from the uploader, list the author's name before the title.)

An e-book

MLA Handbook. 8th ed., e-book, Modern Language Association of America, 2016.

MLA Handbook. 8th ed., Kindle ed., Modern Language Association of America, 2016.

(Note: If you are able to identify the type of e-book, such as Kindle or EPUB, that you consulted, list it instead of "e-book.")

<u>Practice Activity D</u>: Cite the following online sources by using the information provided below. Remember to apply the correct information, punctuation, and formatting, just as the source would appear on a Works Cited page.

1. Provide a complete citation for "The Battle Royal Presentation" in MLA format as it would appear on a Works Cited page by going to the following YouTube video link: https://youtu.be/-CO-wso7IdA.
2. Provide a complete citation for "Is America Any Safer?" by Steven Brill in MLA format as it would appear on a Works Cited page by going to the following online magazine link: www.theatlantic.com/magazine/archive/2016/09/are-we-any-safer/492761/.
3. Provide a complete citation for "Schools' Budget May Be Frozen" by Gary Eason in MLA format as it would appear on a Works Cited page by going to the following online news source link: http://news.bbc.co.uk/2/hi/uk_news/education/2116129.stm.

Forms for other print and nonprint sources

The sources in the next section appear in various formats, such as films, TV shows, music, and so forth, and they may not always follow the exact documentation style demonstrated in this chapter for books, periodicals, or online sources. Nonetheless, you will follow the basic order of author, title of the source, publication date, and any additional information available for citation clarity and usefulness to a reader.

Here is the basic format for these types of sources, as the examples in this section will demonstrate:

Author. Title. Title of container (self-contained if book), Other contributors (translators or editors), Version (edition), Number (vol. and/or no.), Publisher, Publication Date, Location (pages, paragraphs, URL, or DOI). 2nd container's title, Other contributors, Version, Number, Publisher, Publication Date, Location, Date of Access (if applicable).

A podcast

Martin, Rachel. "YA Author Wisdom: Sandra Cisneros." *Weekend Edition Sunday* from NPR, 14 Aug. 2016, www.npr.org/2016/08/14/489964114/ ya-author-wisdom-sandra-cisneros.

A recording (song or album)

CD

Aerosmith. "Livin' on the Edge." *Get a Grip*, Geffen, 1993.

Online album

Aerosmith. "Angel." *Aerosmith—Big Ones*, Geffen, 1994, www.aerosmithsongs. net/6546424/Angel.

(Note: Begin your citation with the name of the artist, composer, or performer for music. Then, place quotation marks around the title of a song, follow with the title of the album in italics, and list the name of the recording manufacturer and then the publication date. However, if the recording label or name of the album are unavailable, you can omit that information, and keep in mind, you may need to refer to the URL for the location of the song or album if it is an online album versus a CD, for instance.)

Live presentation, speeches, lectures, or other oral performance (including conference presentations)

Montrose, Viggo. "Witchcraft and Waking the Dead." Occultism Forum. Fantasy and Horror Writers of America Annual Convention, 31 Oct. 2013, Warwick Allerton Hotel, Chicago.

Film

Scorsese, Martin, director. *Goodfellas*. Warner Brothers, 1990.

A television program (Netflix, Hulu, Google Play)

Cranston, Bryan, performer. *Breaking Bad*. AMC, 2008–2013.

Gilligan, Vince, creator. *Breaking Bad*. AMC, 2008–2013.

(Note: You have the basic format for citing an entire series of a TV show above with emphasis on the creator or a specific performer, but if you want to highlight a specific episode like "Ozymandias" in Breaking Bad, *include that particular information and then list the title of the television program, the distributor, date of distribution, and URL if applicable, as the example below demonstrates.*)

"Ozymandias." *Breaking Bad*, season 5, episode 14, AMC, 15 Sept. 2013. *Netflix*, www.netflix.com/watch/70236426?trackId=13752289&tctx=0%2C13%2Cc71 0a047-6895-45c9-9639-e2e163d9bfa6-45657473.

An interview

Delaney, Burt. Personal interview. 7 Oct. 1998.

Published interviews in print

Daniels, Jim. "The Ultimate Interview with Sue Kaufman." *Warren Review*, vol. 7, no. 4, 1996, pp. 121–36.

Published interviews, online only

Perry, Tyler. Interview by Oprah Winfrey. *O, the Oprah Magazine*, Dec. 2010, www.oprah.com/entertainment/Oprah-Interviews-Tyler-Perry_1. Accessed on 24 Jan. 2011.

Work of art (painting, sculpture, photography)—no online access of image

Popovic, Sava. *A Young Woman Bathing*. 2005, oil on canvas, National Museum of Serbia.

(Note: Identify the artist's name, the title of the artwork in italics, the date of composition, and the medium of the piece along with the name of the institution in which the artwork is housed and the location of the institution if not listed in the name of the institution, such as the Art Institute of Chicago.)

A published dissertation

Drummond, Heather. *A Deconstructive Inquiry into Finnegan's Wake*. 2008. Columbia U, PhD dissertation.

(Note: Cite the author, title, and date of publication for the core elements of a dissertation, and then, as an optional element, identify the institution granting the degree and a description of the work.)

Practice Activity E: Cite the following sources as they would appear on a Works Cited page in MLA format by using the information provided below. Remember to apply correct punctuation and formatting.

1. Apply the correct MLA format for a recording.

    Name of Artist, Composer, or Performer: Beyoncé
    Title of Song: "Sorry"
    Name of Album: *Lemonade*
    Name of Recording Manufacturer: Parkwood Entertainment
    Date of Publication: 2016
    URL: www.beyonce.com/album/lemonade-visual-album/

2. Apply the correct MLA format for artwork (i.e., painting, sculpture, or photograph).

    Name of Artist: Bridget Riley
    Title of the Artwork: *Nataraja*
    Date of Composition: 1993
    Medium of the Piece: oil on canvas
    Name of Institution Housing the Artwork: Tate Modern
    Location of the Institution: London

3. Apply the correct MLA format for a film.

    Title of Film: *Mean Girls*
    Director: Mark S. Waters
    Distributor: Paramount
    Year of Release: 2004

How should you arrange your paper in MLA format?

Format your paper by applying the MLA guidelines listed below. This is just as important as properly documenting your sources in the Works Cited and providing parenthetical citations in your papers. Therefore, the first page of a sample essay follows in order to show you the visual arrangement of a paper in MLA format, along with a practice activity. Here are the guidelines to apply:

- Double-space your whole paper and print it out on standard, white, 8.5 × 11 inch paper.

- Use a legible 12-point font such as Times New Roman and set the margins to 1 inch on all sides of your document.
- Indent the first line of paragraphs about one-half inch (5 spaces) when you use the tab key.
- List your name, your instructor's name, the course, and the date (double-spaced) in the upper left-hand corner of the first page. (Note: The date should be inverted: 15 September 2016.)
- Center the title of your paper without adding extra space between your title and the first paragraph of your paper, and type the title in title case (standard capitalization). In other words, do not italicize, underline, or add quotation marks around the title, since it should match the font style and size of the rest of your document. (Note: Otherwise, use italics throughout your paper for titles of longer works or quotation marks when referring to other works in your titles; for example, The Theme of Revenge in "The Cask of Amontillado".)
- Generate a header in the upper right-hand corner with your last name, a space, and page number, and number all pages consecutively with Arabic numerals (1, 2, 3, etc.) about one-half inch from the top and flush with the right margin. (Note: Follow your instructor's requirements if he or she asks you to omit your last name or even the page number on your first page.)

Sample Paper with MLA Formatting

Doe 1

John Doe

Professor Bailey-Kirby

English 102

15 October 2016

Animal Testing Should Be Banned

With people's increased reliance on advanced medical technology and cosmetic products, animals are used more in testing currently than ever before. According to one study, in the United States alone, "The 2013 USDA Annual Report of Animal Usage documented 85,325 animals that experienced unrelieved pain and distress in fiscal year 2013" (Stokes 1297). Many of these animals are not being treated with the respect and dignity that they deserve. Frequently, these animals are kept locked away and subjected to a wide variety of medicines and treatments that often leave many of them scarred or suffering from other horrific side effects. On top of that, many of the tests done on animals are not even that effective, and a number of better options exist out there. By banning animal testing, the government would end the inhumane treatment of many animals, promote experimentation methods that are more compatible on human beings, and encourage the use of better alternatives.

The first reason to ban animal testing is because it is fundamentally inhumane. Many of the animals kept locked up in these labs are frequently subjected to cruel and often painful experiments that cause them to suffer, and this barbaric practice needs to be made illegal. Wendy Higgins, a writer for The Animals' Agenda, describes the effects of some of these horrific experiments:

Last February the commission published proposals for a new EU chemicals testing policy that relies heavily on immensely cruel toxicity tests on such animals as fish, rats, rabbits, and dogs. These animals will be forced to inhale toxic substances, have chemicals injected into their bloodstream, pumped into their stomach, spread across their shaved and abraded skin, and squirted into their eyes. Fish will have pollutants poured into their water, and pregnant animals will be poisoned to see what mutations develop in their unborn offspring. The chemical poisoning will result in painful sores, burns, internal bleeding, organ damage, cancerous tumors, muscle spasms, nausea, collapse, coma, and eventually death. (13)

This report clearly shows that many animals within these labs are not treated with the respect and dignity that they deserve, which ultimately leads to their needless suffering and even death. Therefore, animal testing should be banned because the animals are not treated properly inside of testing labs.

Practice Activity F: Format a paper for this class or use one from a previous semester to complete this practice activity. This will help you learn to apply the MLA guidelines listed in this chapter as you arrange your heading, margins, and so forth to fit the criteria. Use the sample essay page provided with formatting to aid you in completing this practice activity. When you have revised your paper to meet these MLA guidelines, submit your MLA-formatted paper to your instructor.

1. Double-space your whole paper and print it out on a standard, white, 8.5 × 11 inch paper.
2. Use a legible 12-point font such as Times New Roman and set the margins to 1 inch on all sides of your document.
3. Indent the first line of paragraphs about one-half inch (5 spaces) when you use the tab key.
4. List your name, your instructor's name, the course, and the date (double-spaced) in the upper left-hand corner of the first page. (Note: The date should be inverted: 15 September 2016.)
5. Create a title for your paper and then center it without adding extra space between your title and the first paragraph of your paper, and type the title in title case (standard capitalization), such as the following: The Dangers of Raising the Minimum Wage.
6. Generate a header in the upper right-hand corner with your last name, a space, and page number, and number all pages consecutively with Arabic numerals of (1, 2, 3, etc.) about one-half inch from the top and flush with the right margin.

CHAPTER 4
ARGUMENT

Figure 4.1   Three Presidents' Logical Fallacies Cartoon

In this chapter, you will learn about writing an argument. Most of your college papers will require you to take a stance on a controversial issue or a social problem with the purpose of persuading your audience to accept your side. Hence, it is important to understand the elements of argument that you will need to apply in your writing; these tactics include claim, support, and assumptions, along with the three appeals of ethos, pathos, and logos. Besides learning these components for a more credible and logical argument, you will review deductive reasoning and inductive reasoning as well as how to identify and avoid logical fallacies in your writing in this chapter's sequence of practice activities.

ELEMENTS OF ARGUMENT

WHAT ARE THE ELEMENTS OF ARGUMENT?

The elements of argument include the three main parts of *claim*, which refers to your position or the conclusion of your argument; *support*, which involves the grounds for your argument or reasons, data, and evidence to back your claim; and *warrant*, which is your argument's assumption or principle that links your reasons to your claim. The three subdivisions are as follows: *backing*, which entails the justifications for the warrant; *rebuttal*, which concerns counterexamples, the opposing side's reservations, and exceptions to the claim; and *qualifier*, which indicates the degree of limitations or restrictions to claim, warrant, and backing.

These six segments are known as the Toulmin method, for the twentieth-century British philosopher Stephen Toulmin, who wanted to establish a straightforward technique for everyday logical and pragmatic arguments. His mode's purpose is meant to assist you in analyzing an argument you are reading, so you will be able to understand how an argument works as well as be able to organize and structure an effective argument of your own with more confidence.

HOW DO YOU UTILIZE THESE ELEMENTS OF ARGUMENT?

You will first need to consider what sort of topic interests you before you can write an argument paper. It should be a subject that you care about, are willing to examine from multiple viewpoints, and able to research efficiently in the time allotted for the assignment. Furthermore, your campus or local public library might have a Web site with a link to debatable topics or opposing viewpoints that catalogs issues and counterperspective articles to help you decide on a topic.

If not, you may want to look at one of the 125 topics listed in the chart that follows, such as minimum wage or vaccines/vaccinations. Of course, there are hundreds of other areas you could explore besides the items provided in the chart. However, you may want to begin with one of these topics and ask yourself: Should we increase the minimum wage? Should children receive mandatory vaccinations? Then, you can expand the scope of your interests from there.

Your topic might be a social issue or one on the environment, education, technology, immigration, the military, media, or even race, culture, and identity. If you are not sure about choosing a topic, you might want to review the first chapter's suggestions on generating ideas, such as brainstorming a list of topics, freewriting, or jotting down a few journalistic questions.

Once you have selected a debatable issue, decide on a *claim (of fact, cause, value, or policy)*. As stated earlier, your claim is your position or the conclusion of your argument. You may want to begin with the following questions, in order to formulate a claim: What is my thesis? What do I want to prove? What do I want my audience to believe/know/think about _____? An example claim could involve the following: *The US government should ban GMOs.* Below is a more comprehensive list for the main types of claims to help you understand the idea better.

TYPES OF CLAIMS

- **Claim of Fact:** This is also known as claim of definition, and it makes a supposition about the past, present, or future. It also requires sufficient proof from a credible authority, accurate data presented as support, and terms that are clearly defined. The questions to contemplate include the following when framing your thoughts into a succinct claim: What happened? Is it true? Does it exist? What is it? How should we classify or define it?

    Example: Standardized tests are an insufficient barometer of a student's intelligence.

Debatable Topics

1. 9/11 Attacks
2. Abortion: Late-Term/Partial-Birth
3. Advertising
4. Affirmative Action
5. AIDS
6. Alcoholism
7. Alternative Medicine
8. Alzheimer's Disease
9. Animal Experimentation/Testing
10. Animal Rights
11. Artificial Intelligence
12. Assisted Suicide
13. Atheism
14. Attention-Deficit/Hyperactivity Disorder (ADHD)
15. Autism
16. Behavioral Disorders
17. Biofuels
18. Body Image
19. Cancer Risks
20. Capital Punishment
21. Carbon Offsets
22. Censorship
23. Child Abuse
24. Civil Rights
25. Climate Change
26. Cloning
27. Concealed Weapons
28. Conspiracy Theories
29. Creationism
30. Cults
31. Cyberbullying
32. Cybercrime
33. Depression
34. Dietary Supplements/ Dieting
35. Digitizing Books
36. Domestic Violence
37. DREAM Act
38. Drug Abuse
39. Drug Legalization
40. Drugs and Athletes
41. Drunk Driving
42. Eating Disorders
43. Education
44. Emigration and Immigration
45. Energy Crisis
46. Environmentalism
47. Evolution
48. Factory Farming
49. Feminism
50. Food Insecurity
51. Food Safety
52. Foreign Oil Dependence
53. Fracking
54. Free Trade
55. Freedom of Speech
56. Gangs
57. Gay Parents
58. Gays in the Military
59. Gendercide
60. Genetic Disorders
61. Genetic Engineering
62. Genetically Modified Food
63. Global Warming
64. Globalization
65. Gun Control
66. Guns and Violence
67. Hacking and Hackers
68. Hate Crimes
69. Health Care Issues
70. Homelessness
71. Homeschooling
72. Homosexuality
73. Human Genetics
74. Human Rights
75. Human Trafficking
76. Hybrid and Electric Cars
77. Illegal Immigrants
78. Infectious Diseases
79. Iraq Wars
80. Islamic Fundamentalism
81. Medicare
82. Mental Disorders
83. Mental Health
84. Minimum Wage
85. Nanotechnology
86. NASA
87. Nuclear Energy/Safety
88. Obesity
89. Offshore Drilling
90. Online Social Media/Networks
91. Organic Food
92. Outsourcing
93. Pollution
94. Polygamy
95. Pornography
96. Post-Traumatic Stress Disorder (PTSD)
97. Poverty
98. Prescription Medication Abuse
99. Prostitution
100. Racial Profiling/Racism
101. Recycling
102. Renewable Energy
103. Right to Bear Arms
104. Same-Sex Marriage
105. Sex Education
106. Sexting
107. Sexually Transmitted Diseases
108. Slavery Reparations
109. Smoking
110. Social Security
111. Space Exploration
112. Special Education and Learning Disabilities
113. Standardized Testing
114. Sweatshops
115. Terrorism
116. Texting while Driving
117. Transgender People
118. Vaccines/Vaccinations
119. Vegetarianism
120. Video Games & Violence
121. Wage Discrimination
122. War Crimes
123. Welfare Reform
124. Women's Rights
125. Zero Tolerance Policies

- **Claim of Cause (and Effect):** This is akin to the claim of fact (or definition), and it needs to be opinionated and debatable as well as include the same sort of proof as a claim of fact. However, there tends to be more of a causal connection, predictive reference in the statement, or origin/root versus consequence/outcome relationship. As a result, bear in mind the following questions to aid you in verbalizing a concisely worded claim: What caused it? What are the effects? Why did it happen? What are the results short and long term?

  Example: Spending more than five hours on social media per day seems to trigger an increase in depression and anxiety in teenagers.
- **Claim of Value:** This evaluates and judges between the merits of opposing morals or tastes, and its proof requires the use of an evaluation system with a set of clear criteria, reliable authorities for evidence, and illustrations and other examples to shed light on any abstract concepts. Thus, the questions to reflect on might involve these sorts of questions when

articulating your claim of value: Is it good or bad? Moral or immoral? Ethical or unethical? Valuable or not valuable?

>   **Example:** Animal testing is unethical.

- **Claim of Policy:** This ascertains the kind of change in behavior, education, law, and/or policy that needs to be taken with a proposed solution or call to action, uses "should" or "ought" statements for its resolution, and might include possible subclaims of fact or value in the statement. Similarly, its proof needs to involve a workable plan for a realistic course of action, consider the counterarguments, and deem the advantages or justifications for a specific call to action. In the end, the questions might consist of the following: What should we do about this dilemma? How should we solve this problem? What is the cure for this crisis?

>   **Example:** The US welfare system should be reformed (argues for a solution/policy) since it does not sufficiently assist American families below the poverty line (fact).

Practice Activity A: Identify each of the statements below as a claim of fact, cause, value, or policy, and then justify your classification briefly for each one.

1. The oldest known profession in the world is prostitution.
2. The Chicago Bulls are the best team in the NBA.
3. Congress should decrease the drinking age to sixteen.
4. Global warming is produced by carbon emissions.
5. Chipotle is a much healthier eatery than Taco Bell.
6. There is a God.
7. The US government should provide free college education for all students.
8. The effects of radiation poisoning can be explained by the recent leak at the nuclear plant.
9. The growth of the tobacco industry in the twentieth century led to an overall increase in lung cancer.
10. Christian Bale's performance as Batman was far better than that of any other actors.

Once you have a clear idea for your claim, determine the **warrant** or principle assumption. This is not usually stated directly like the other attributes of an argument, but it can be based on ethos, logos, or pathos for your argument. These three modes of persuasion will be reviewed later in this chapter; in the meantime, if you refer to the claim above (i.e., The US government should ban GMOs), your warrant might be: *The US government should protect the health of its citizens.* Therefore, you might ask yourself: What values do I hold that make me choose a position like banning GMOs or making them illegal? What is my underlying assumption that connects the grounds to my claim? Does my audience agree or disagree with me? How can I encourage all parties to share similar viewpoints?

Afterward, make an inference by establishing the **grounds** or evidence and support. Address the following: What concrete facts, reasons, or data will support my claim? Keeping with the same topic of GMOs, you might make the following statement for your grounds: *Banning GMOs would protect the health of US citizens.* (Notice the breakdown for the claim, warrant/

assumption, and ground/support outlined below for the initial steps to form your argument. When the warrant and grounds are true, the claim must be true and effective as well.)

Example Steps for Claim, Warrant, and Grounds

	A: Responsible party	B: Action to be taken
Claim:	The US government **should ban GMOs.**	
	Repeat "A" in warrant	C: Value
Warrant:	The US government **should** protect the health of its citizens.	
	Repeat "B" in grounds	Repeat "C" in grounds
Grounds:	Banning GMOs **would** protect the health of US citizens.	
	(Note: Use will or would, *not* should, *in the third step.*)	

Next, you will need **backing,** in which you give additional evidence, reasons, and justifications to support the warrant with "since" or "because" clauses, typically before the supplementary proof: *Research shows that mammals fed GMOs have their immune systems compromised; their organs (kidneys, liver, adrenal glands, spleen, and heart) damaged; and even their brain size reduced in some cases.* However, when you provide backing, you must ask yourself: Who is my audience? What similar warrants does my audience have with me? What additional evidence exists to support my warrant?

Then, you must tackle the **qualifiers,** since they propose the constraints of the argument or conditions in which the argument is probable, accurate, and verifiable, such as the following: *If there isn't any evidence to the contrary, GMOs are likely to harm an individual's well-being.* Once again, you may need to make an inquiry, in order to comprehend the level of restrictions to your claim, warrant, grounds, and backing. Your thoughtful response to the following questions can abet any limitations to your argument; hence, you may want to revise the wording of your argument: How convincing is my argument? Should I assert my argument in probable terms, such as *possibly, usually, sometimes, mostly, likely, if,* and *probably,* or in more absolute terms like *never* or *always*?

Moreover, you might need to clarify the **rebuttal,** or in other words, as stated earlier, the opposing side's reservations, doubts, or other exceptions to the claim. Keep in mind, any rebuttal is an argument in itself. Hence, it might include a claim, warrant, backing, and so forth and often introduce the opposing side's qualms with "Unless," "Although," or "Even though" clauses, as shown in this example: *Although regulatory agencies like the USDA, FDA, and EPA must oversee and approve GMO crops as safe before any potential product is sold to farmers, consumers, or any country, banning GMOs would protect the health of US citizens, since research shows that mammals fed GMOs have their immune systems compromised; their organs (kidneys, liver, adrenal glands, spleen, and heart) damaged; and even their brain size reduced in many cases.* Likewise, for the rebuttal, you will want to pose a query to understand the opponent's side and assuage any misgivings: What are the other opinions on this issue? How should I explain that, so my stance is stronger? Which of these different viewpoints will I need to address in my paper?

Finally, learning these terms is not an end in itself, but it serves the purpose of helping you read another's argument and organize your understanding of it with Toulmin's language. In some cases, when you are asked to analyze an essay's argument, you may find that there are no rebuttals or qualifiers, since some arguments are absolutes. However, being able to distinguish what the claim, warrant, grounds, and backing are will still aid you in improving your critical-thinking skills by evaluating the argument.

Example of the Complete Argument with Toulmin's System

In order to protect the health of its citizens, the US government should ban GMOs, as they are likely to harm an individual's well-being, because research shows that mammals fed GMOs have their immune systems compromised, their organs damaged, and even their brain size reduced in many cases, although regulatory agencies like the USDA, FDA, and EPA must oversee and approve GMO crops as safe before any potential product is sold to farmers, consumers, or any country.

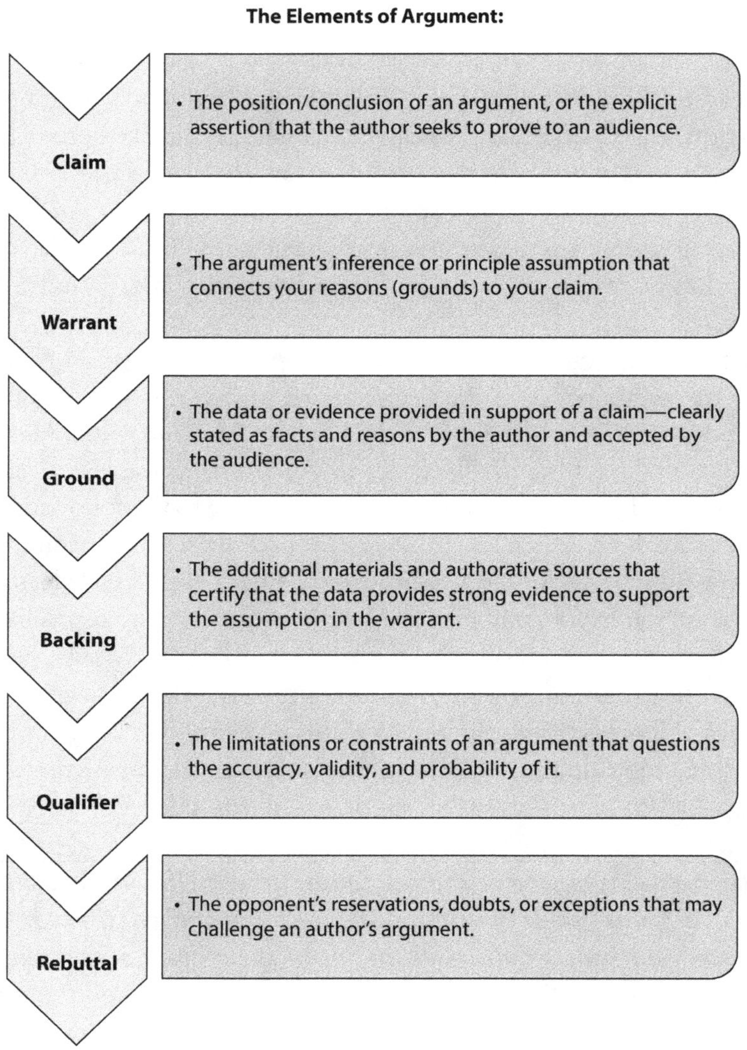

The Elements of Argument:

Claim
- The position/conclusion of an argument, or the explicit assertion that the author seeks to prove to an audience.

Warrant
- The argument's inference or principle assumption that connects your reasons (grounds) to your claim.

Ground
- The data or evidence provided in support of a claim—clearly stated as facts and reasons by the author and accepted by the audience.

Backing
- The additional materials and authorative sources that certify that the data provides strong evidence to support the assumption in the warrant.

Qualifier
- The limitations or constraints of an argument that questions the accuracy, validity, and probability of it.

Rebuttal
- The opponent's reservations, doubts, or exceptions that may challenge an author's argument.

Figure 4.2

Read Harold LeClair Ickes's "Call for What Is an American" and answer the questions that follow. This next practice activity will help you reflect on the reading and develop your critical-thinking skills by carefully considering what his argument is about, how he engages the audience, and why his speech has historical significance.

CALL FOR WHAT IS AN AMERICAN BY HAROLD LECLAIR ICKES

This remarkable speech was delivered during an I Am an American Day gathering in New York's Central Park by Harold Ickes, President Franklin Roosevelt's secretary of the interior. It came at a perilous moment in history, May 1941, when Adolf Hitler and the Nazis seemed headed toward possible world domination.

By this time, countries that had fallen to the Nazis included Austria, Czechoslovakia, Poland, Norway, Denmark, France, Belgium, Luxembourg, the Netherlands, and areas in North Africa. Airfields and cities in England were now under ferocious air attack from the German Luftwaffe, while wolf packs of Nazi U-boats attempted to blockade the British Isles.

Many Americans, however, still questioned the wisdom and necessity of direct US involvement in the European war. Pacifist sentiment was steadily growing, while at the same time Fascism was sometimes referred to as the "wave of the future" by respected Americans, buoyed in part by the ceaseless barrage of highly effective antidemocratic propaganda emanating from the Fascist countries of Europe, including Germany.

In this speech, Harold Ickes counters that propaganda, defines what it means to be a free American, and offers a blunt assessment of the perilous future the United States would face standing alone against a victorious Hitler.

———

I want to ask a few simple questions. And then I shall answer them.

What has happened to our vaunted idealism? Why have some of us been behaving like scared chickens? Where is the million-throated, democratic voice of America?

For years it has been dinned into us that we are a weak nation; that we are an inefficient people; that we are simple-minded. For years we have been told that we are beaten, decayed, and that no part of the world belongs to us any longer.

Some amongst us have fallen for this carefully pickled tripe. Some amongst us have fallen for this calculated poison. Some amongst us have begun to preach that the "wave of the future" has passed over us and left us a wet, dead fish.

They shout—from public platforms in printed pages, through the microphones—that it is futile to oppose the "wave of the future." They cry that we Americans, we free Americans nourished on Magna Carta and the Declaration of Independence, hold moth-eaten ideas. They exclaim that there is no room for free men in the world any more and that only the slaves will inherit the earth. America—the America of Washington and Jefferson and Lincoln and Walt Whitman—they say, is waiting for the undertaker and all the hopes and aspirations that have gone into the making of America are dead too.

However, my fellow citizens, this is not the real point of the story. The real point—the shameful point—is that many of us are listening to them and some of us almost believe them.

I say that it is time for the great American people to raise its voice and cry out in mighty triumph what it is to be an American. And why it is that only Americans, with the aid of our brave allies—yes, let's call them "allies"—the British, can and will build the only future worth having. I mean a future, not of concentration camps, not of physical torture and mental straitjackets, not of sawdust bread or of sawdust Caesars—I mean a future when free men will live free lives in dignity and in security.

This tide of the future, the democratic future, is ours. It is ours if we show ourselves worthy of our culture and of our heritage.

But make no mistake about it; the tide of the democratic future is not like the ocean tide—regular, relentless, and inevitable. Nothing in human affairs is mechanical or inevitable. Nor are Americans mechanical. They are very human indeed.

What constitutes an American? Not color nor race nor religion. Not the pedigree of his family nor the place of his birth. Not the coincidence of his citizenship. Not his social status nor his bank account. Not his trade nor his profession. An American is one who loves justice and believes in the dignity of man. An American is one who will fight for his freedom and that of his neighbor. An American is one who will sacrifice property, ease and security in order that he and his children may retain the rights of free men. An American is one in whose heart is engraved the immortal second sentence of the Declaration of Independence.

Americans have always known how to fight for their rights and their way of life. Americans are not afraid to fight. They fight joyously in a just cause.

We Americans know that freedom, like peace, is indivisible. We cannot retain our liberty if three-fourths of the world is enslaved. Brutality, injustice and slavery, if practiced as dictators would have them, universally and systematically, in the long run would destroy us as surely as a fire raging in our nearby neighbor's house would burn ours if we didn't help to put out his.

If we are to retain our own freedom, we must do everything within our power to aid Britain. We must also do everything to restore to the conquered peoples their freedom. This means the Germans too.

Such a program, if you stop to think, is selfishness on our part. It is the sort of enlightened selfishness that makes the wheels of history go around. It is the sort of enlightened selfishness that wins victories.

Do you know why? Because we cannot live in the world alone, without friends and without allies. If Britain should be defeated, then the totalitarian undertaker will prepare to hang crepe on the door of our own independence.

Perhaps you wonder how this could come about? Perhaps you have heard "them"—the wavers of the future—cry, with calculated malice, that even if Britain were defeated we could live alone and defend ourselves single handed, even against the whole world.

I tell you that this is a cold blooded lie.

We would be alone in the world, facing an unscrupulous military-economic bloc that would dominate all of Europe, all of Africa, most of Asia, and perhaps even Russia and South America. Even to do that, we would have to spend most of our national income on tanks and guns and planes and ships. Nor would this be all. We would have to live perpetually as an armed camp, maintaining a huge standing army, a gigantic air force, two vast navies. And we could not do this without endangering our freedom, our democracy, our way of life.

Perhaps such is the America "they"—the wavers of the future—foresee. Perhaps such is the America that a certain aviator, with his contempt for democracy, would prefer. Perhaps such is the America that a certain Senator desires. Perhaps such is the America that a certain mail order executive longs for.

But a perpetually militarized, isolated and impoverished America is not the America that our fathers came here to build.

It is not the America that has been the dream and the hope of countless generations in all parts of the world. It is not the America that one hundred and thirty million of us would care to live in.

The continued security of our country demands that we aid the enslaved millions of Europe—yes, even of Germany—to win back their liberty and independence. I am convinced that if we do not embark upon such a program we will lose our own freedom.

We should be clear on this point. What is convulsing the world today is not merely another old-fashioned war. It is a counter revolution against our ideas and ideals, against our sense of justice and our human values.

Three systems today compete for world domination. Communism, fascism, and democracy are struggling for social-economic-political world control. As the conflict sharpens, it becomes clear that the other two, fascism and communism, are merging into one. They have one common enemy, democracy. They have one common goal, the destruction of democracy.

This is why this war is not an ordinary war. It is not a conflict for markets or territories. It is a desperate struggle for the possession of the souls of men.

This is why the British are not fighting for themselves alone. They are fighting to preserve freedom for mankind. For the moment, the battleground is the British Isles. But they are fighting our war; they are the first soldiers in trenches that are also our front-line trenches.

In this world war of ideas and of loyalties we believers in democracy must do two things. We must unite our forces to form one great democratic international. We must offer a clear program to freedom-loving peoples throughout the world.

Freedom-loving men and women in every land must organize and tighten their ranks. The masses everywhere must be helped to fight their oppressors and conquerors.

We, free, democratic Americans are in a position to help. We know that the spirit of freedom never dies. We know that men have fought and bled for freedom since time immemorial. We realize that the liberty-loving German people are only temporarily enslaved. We do not doubt that the Italian people are looking forward to the appearance of another Garibaldi. We know how the Poles have for centuries maintained a heroic resistance against tyranny. We remember the brave struggle of the Hungarians under Kossuth and other leaders. We recall the heroic figure of Masaryk and the gallant fight for freedom of the Czech people. The story of the Yugoslavs', especially the Serbs' blows for liberty and independence is a saga of extraordinary heroism. The Greeks will stand again at Thermopylae, as they have in the past. The annals of our American sister-republics, too, are glorious with freedom-inspiring exploits. The noble figure of Simon Bolivar, the great South American liberator, has naturally been compared with that of George Washington.

No, liberty never dies. The Genghis Khans come and go. The Attilas come and go. The Hitlers flash and sputter out. But freedom endures.

Destroy a whole generation of those who have known how to walk with heads erect in God's free air, and the next generation will rise against the oppressors and restore freedom. Today in Europe, the Nazi Attila may gloat that he has destroyed democracy. He is wrong. In small farmhouses all over Central Europe, in the shops of Germany and Italy, on the docks of Holland and Belgium, freedom still lives in the hearts of men. It will endure like a hardy tree gone into the wintertime, awaiting the spring.

And, like spring, spreading from the South into Scandinavia, the democratic revolution will come. And men with democratic hearts will experience comradeship across artificial boundaries.

These men and women, hundreds of millions of them, now in bondage or threatened with slavery, are our comrades and our allies. They are only waiting for our leadership and our encouragement, for the spark that we can supply.

These hundreds of millions, of liberty-loving people, now oppressed, constitute the greatest sixth column in history. They have the will to destroy the Nazi gangsters.

We have always helped in struggles for human freedom. And we will help again. But our hundreds of millions of liberty-loving allies would despair if we did not provide aid and encouragement. The quicker we help them the sooner this dreadful revolution will be over. We cannot, we must not, we dare not delay much longer.

The fight for Britain is in its crucial stages. We must give the British everything we have. And by everything, I mean everything needed to beat the life out of our common enemy.

The second step must be to aid and encourage our friends and allies everywhere. And by everywhere I mean Europe and Asia and Africa and America.

And finally, the most important of all, we Americans must gird spiritually for the battle. We must dispel the fog of uncertainty and vacillation. We must greet with raucous laughter the corroding arguments of our appeasers and fascists. They doubt democracy. We affirm it triumphantly so that all the world may hear:

Here in America we have something so worth living for that it is worth dying for! The so-called "wave of the future" is but the slimy backwash of the past. We have not heaved from our necks the tyrant's crushing heel, only to stretch our necks out again for its weight. Not only will we fight for democracy, we will make it more worth fighting for. Under our free institutions, we will work for the good of mankind, including Hitler's victims in Germany, so that all may have plenty and security.

We American democrats know that when good will prevails among men there will be a world of plenty and a world of security.

In the words of Winston Churchill, "Are we downhearted," No, we are not! But someone is downhearted! Witness the terrified flight of Hess, Hitler's Number Three Man. And listen to this—listen carefully:

"The British nation can be counted upon to carry through to victory any struggle that it once enters upon no matter how long such a struggle may last or however great the sacrifices that may be necessary or whatever the means that have to be employed; and all this even though the actual military equipment at hand may be utterly inadequate when compared with that of other nations."

Do you know who wrote that? Adolf Hitler in Mein Kampf. And do you know who took down that dictation? Rudolf Hess.

We will help to make Hitler's prophecy come true. We will help brave England drive back the hordes from Hell who besiege her and then we will join for the destruction of savage and blood-thirsty dictators everywhere. But we must be firm and decisive. We must know our will and make it felt. And we must hurry.

Harold Ickes, May 18, 1941

Practice Activity B: Read "Call for What Is an American" by Harold LeClair Ickes and answer the questions that follow in complete sentences. Be prepared to share your response with your peers and instructor during a class discussion.

1. What is Harold Ickes arguing? Identify his claim, warrant(s), grounds, backing for warrants, rebuttal, and qualifier. Follow the steps below and reply to each question to help you understand their argument.
    a. For the claim, what does the author want you to believe?
    b. For the warrant(s), why is this claim important to the author? What are the author's assumptions?
    c. For the grounds, why should you believe the author, or what evidence does he offer?

Continued

    d. For the backing of warrants, what additional support does the author give, in order to remind you of the warrants and make you want to agree with him?

    e. For the rebuttal, are there any other counterexamples or positions shown? Are they contested or addressed by the author?

    f. For the qualifier, is there any indication that the claim might be limited (*sometimes, probably, possibly, if*)?

2. How does he engage the audience from the start? What is the tone of his speech?

3. For what purpose does he say, "We cannot retain our liberty if three-fourths of the world is enslaved" in paragraph 12? What does he mean by this?

4. What is the historical significance of this document? What was happening in the United States during this time that makes this a relevant argument?

5. Do you find his argument convincing? Why or why not?

THE APPEALS OF ARGUMENT: ETHOS, PATHOS, AND LOGOS

WHAT ARE THE APPEALS OF ARGUMENT?

The Greek philosopher Aristotle argued that there are three basic appeals for persuading an audience of your position: ethos, logos, and pathos. These modes work best when they are used together for writing a position paper or giving a speech, in order to make a convincing argument. By understanding the framework of each one with the definitions and examples provided, you will be able to apply them effectively.

Ethos refers to the speaker's character or ethics as listeners perceive them. If their impression is that a speaker has a good moral character, they are predisposed to assume that the speaker is credible. The speaker should also appear to be a knowledgeable authority, reliable proponent, or expert on the subject. Witness how John F. Kennedy displays ethos in the excerpt from his "State of the Union Message" and carefully consider what values or principles are conveyed.

Example of Ethos

I have pledged myself and my colleagues in the cabinet to a continuous encouragement of initiative, responsibility and energy in serving the public interest. Let every public servant know, whether his post is high or low, that a man's rank and reputation in this Administration will be determined by the size of the job he does, and not by the size of his staff, his office or his budget.... And let every man and woman who works in any area of our national government, in any branch, at any level, be able to say with pride and with honor in future years: "I served the United States Government in that hour of our nation's need."

—Excerpt taken from John F. Kennedy's State of the Union
Message, January 30, 1961

Logos, on the other hand, involves a more rhetorical type of reasoning, since it uses facts and evidence to sway a reader on the strengths of the argument. This appeal to reason and logic stems from Aristotle's formal arguments based on what he identifies as syllogisms.

For instance, a syllogism is a sort of logical discourse of suppositions that arrive at a conclusion or inference based on a major and minor proposition, such as "All women like to dance (major premise). Mary is a woman (minor premise). Therefore, Mary must like to dance (conclusion)."

In other words, the two types of reasoning that Aristotle discusses are deductive and inductive reasoning. Deductive reasoning explains the way of thinking or logic used when you come to a conclusion about a specific circumstance from general statements like the example above. Another model of logos is provided in the excerpt below.

Example of Logos

Two major studies from military intelligence experts have warned our leaders about the dangerous national security implications of the climate crisis, including the possibility of hundreds of millions of climate refugees destabilizing nations around the world. Just two days ago, 27 senior statesmen and retired military leaders warned of the national security threat from an "energy tsunami" that would be triggered by a loss of our access to foreign oil. Meanwhile, the war in Iraq continues, and now the war in Afghanistan appears to be getting worse.

—Excerpt taken from Al Gore's "A Generational Challenge
to Repower America," July 17, 2008

However, inductive reasoning is quite the opposite, since you select a few specific cases or occurrences and lead to broader conclusions. To illustrate this point, inductive reasoning might suggest the following: "I know several middle-aged men who have tattoos. Therefore, every middle-aged man has at least one tattoo."

Although this type of reasoning may result in logical fallacies that will be reviewed later in this chapter, it can be compelling when applied correctly with judicious reasons to persuade an audience to your position. Thus, it will be important for you to learn to identify logical fallacies in order to avoid any discrepancy in logic in your arguments.

Conversely, *pathos* entails a petition to the emotions or passions of an individual. An author may use language to evoke a certain feeling or reaction about an issue in his or her audience. By eliciting readers' compassion and sympathy, you can inspire them to action and even persuade them to your side if you know their state of mind or what motivates them. See how pathos is employed by Barack Obama in the excerpt below.

Example of Pathos

This country is more generous than one where a man in Indiana has to pack up the equipment he's worked on for twenty years and watch it shipped off to China, and then chokes up as he explains how he felt like a failure when he went home to tell his family the news.

We are more compassionate than a government that lets veterans sleep on our streets and families slide into poverty; that sits on its hands while a major American city drowns before our eyes.

—Excerpt taken from Barack Obama's "Night Before the
Election Speech," Manassas, Prince William County,
Virginia, November 3, 2008

The Appeals of Argument:

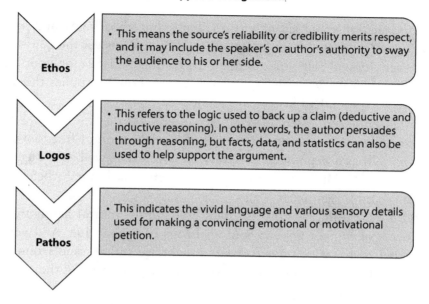

Figure 4.3

Practice Activity C: Identify which type of appeal is being used in the examples below, and justify your choice with a brief explanation (at least one sentence) for each one.

1. "As a lawyer who earned a degree from Yale University and has practiced law for more than a decade, I am more than qualified to advise you to take the settlement as the best outcome in this lawsuit."

2. Abortions should be permitted by law under any circumstances since the majority of Americans support them, according to the May 2014 Harvard Research poll that shows 54% of Americans support a woman's right to an abortion.

3. "The nighttime sniffling, sneezing, coughing, aching, stuffy head fever so you can rest medicine" (NyQuil).

4. "I've been a general in the United States Army for the past fourteen years, did my first tour in Vietnam, and served more than fifty years in a successful military career, so you can trust me when I say that I will bring back our American boys safe and sound from Afghanistan."

5. The data in the ten-year study demonstrate an average ten-pound increase in weight loss for four out of five women who used the new supplement for more than a month, compared to the group who took the placebo with no significant changes at all.

JOHN F. KENNEDY'S INAUGURAL ADDRESS ON JANUARY 20, 1961

Once you have completed the practice activity on identifying ethos, logos, and pathos, read John F. Kennedy's "Inaugural Address" from January 20, 1961, and answer the questions that follow. This next practice activity will help you reflect on the reading and develop your critical-thinking skills by carefully considering what his argument is about, how he applies the three appeals of argument, and why his speech had historical significance.

We observe today not a victory of party but a celebration of freedom ... symbolizing an end as well as a beginning ... signifying renewal as well as change for I have sworn before you and Almighty God the same solemn oath our forbears prescribed nearly a century and three-quarters ago.

The world is very different now, for man holds in his mortal hands the power to abolish all forms of human poverty and all forms of human life. And yet the same revolutionary beliefs for which our forbears fought are still at issue around the globe ... the belief that the rights of man come not from the generosity of the state but from the hand of God. We dare not forget today that we are the heirs of that first revolution.

Let the word go forth from this time and place ... to friend and foe alike ... that the torch has been passed to a new generation of Americans ... born in this century, tempered by war, disciplined by a hard and bitter peace, proud of our ancient heritage ... and unwilling to witness or permit the slow undoing of those human rights to which this nation has always been committed, and to which we are committed today ... at home and around the world.

Let every nation know ... whether it wishes us well or ill ... that we shall pay any price, bear any burden, meet any hardship, support any friend, oppose any foe, to assure the survival and the success of liberty. This much we pledge ... and more.

To those old allies whose cultural and spiritual origins we share: we pledge the loyalty of faithful friends. United ... there is little we cannot do in a host of co-operative ventures. Divided ... there is little we can do ... for we dare not meet a powerful challenge, at odds, and split asunder. To those new states whom we welcome to the ranks of the free: we pledge our word that one form of colonial control shall not have passed away merely to be replaced by a far more iron tyranny. We shall not always expect to find them supporting our view. But we shall always hope to find them strongly supporting their own freedom ... and to remember that ... in the past ... those who foolishly sought power by riding the back of the tiger ended up inside. To those people in the huts and villages of half the globe struggling to break the bonds of mass misery: we pledge our best efforts to help them help themselves, for whatever period is required ... not because the Communists may be doing it, not because we seek their votes, but because it is right. If a free society cannot help the many who are poor, it cannot save the few who are rich.

To our sister republics south of our border: we offer a special pledge ... to convert our good words into good deeds ... in a new alliance for progress ... to assist free men and free governments in casting off the chains of poverty. But this peaceful revolution of hope cannot become the prey of hostile powers. Let all our neighbors know that we shall join with them to oppose aggression or subversion anywhere in the Americas ...

and let every other power know that this hemisphere intends to remain the master of its own house.

To that world assembly of sovereign states: the United Nations ... our last best hope in an age where the instruments of war have far outpaced the instruments of peace, we renew our pledge of support ... to prevent it from becoming merely a forum for invective ... to strengthen its shield of the new and the weak ... and to enlarge the area in which its writ may run.

Finally, to those nations who would make themselves our adversaries, we offer not a pledge but a request: that both sides begin anew the quest for peace; before the dark powers of destruction unleashed by science engulf all humanity in planned or accidental self-destruction. We dare not tempt them with weakness. For only when our arms are sufficient beyond doubt can we be certain beyond doubt that they will never be employed. But neither can two great and powerful groups of nations take comfort from our present course ... both sides overburdened by the cost of modern weapons, both rightly alarmed by the steady spread of the deadly atom, yet both racing to alter that uncertain balance of terror that stays the hand of Mankind's final war.

So let us begin anew ... remembering on both sides that civility is not a sign of weakness, and sincerity is always subject to proof. Let us never negotiate out of fear, but let us never fear to negotiate. Let both sides explore what problems unite us instead of belaboring those problems which divide us. Let both sides, for the first time, formulate serious and precise proposals for the inspection and control of arms ... and bring the absolute power to destroy other nations under the absolute control of all nations. Let both sides seek to invoke the wonders of science instead of its terrors. Together let us explore the stars, conquer the deserts, eradicate disease, tap the ocean depths, and encourage the arts and commerce. Let both sides unite to heed in all corners of the earth the command of Isaiah ... to "undo the heavy burdens ... let the oppressed go free."

And if a beachhead of co-operation may push back the jungle of suspicion ... let both sides join in creating not a new balance of power ... but a new world of law ... where the strong are just ... and the weak secure ... and the peace preserved....

All this will not be finished in the first one hundred days. Nor will it be finished in the first one thousand days ... nor in the life of this administration, nor even perhaps in our lifetime on this planet. But let us begin.

In your hands, my fellow citizens ... more than mine ... will rest the final success or failure of our course. Since this country was founded, each generation of Americans has been summoned to give testimony to its national loyalty. The graves of young Americans who answered the call to service surround the globe. Now the trumpet summons us again ... not as a call to bear arms, though arms we need ... not as a call to battle ... though embattled we are ... but a call to bear the burden of a long twilight struggle ... year in and year out, rejoicing in hope, patient in tribulation ... a struggle against the common enemies of man: tyranny ... poverty ... disease ... and war itself. Can we forge against these enemies a grand and global alliance ... North and South ... East and West ... that can assure a more fruitful life for all mankind?

Will you join in that historic effort?

In the long history of the world, only a few generations have been granted the role of defending freedom in its hour of maximum danger; I do not shrink from this responsibility ... I welcome it. I do not believe that any of us would exchange places with any other people or any other generation. The energy, the faith, the devotion which we bring to this endeavor will light our country and all who serve it ... and the glow from that fire can truly light the world.

And so, my fellow Americans ... ask not what your country can do for you ... ask what you can do for your country. My fellow citizens of the world ... ask not what America will do for you, but what together we can do for the Freedom of Man.

Finally, whether you are citizens of America or citizens of the world, ask of us here the same high standards of strength and sacrifice which we ask of you. With a good conscience our only sure reward, with history the final judge of our deeds; let us go forth to lead the land we love, asking His blessing and His help, but knowing that here on earth God's work must truly be our own.

Practice Activity D: Answer the questions that follow in complete sentences and be prepared to share your response with your peers and instructor during the class discussion.

1. What is John F. Kennedy arguing? Identify his claim, warrant(s), grounds, backing for warrants, rebuttal, and qualifier. Follow the steps below and reply to each question to help you understand his argument.
   a. For the claim, what does the author want you to believe?
   b. For the warrant(s), why is this claim important to the author? What are the author's assumptions?
   c. For the grounds, why should you believe the author, or what evidence does he offer?
   d. For the backing of warrants, what additional support does the author give, in order to remind you of the warrants and make you want to agree with him?
   e. For the rebuttal, are there any other counterexamples or positions shown? Are they contested or addressed by the author?
   f. For the qualifier, is there any indication that the claim might be limited (*sometimes, probably, possibly, if*)?
2. How does he appeal to ethos (the writer's perceived character), logos (logic), and pathos (emotional quality) with his argument?
3. How does he use the rhetorical devices of triad (three parallel words, phrases, or clauses) and chiasmus (repetition of the same words or an inverted parallelism between two similar phrases or ideas, such as "One should work to live, not live to work")? What purpose does it serve?
4. What is the historical significance of this document? What was happening in the United States during this time that makes this a relevant argument?
5. Do you find his argument convincing? Why or why not?

LOGICAL FALLACIES

WHAT ARE LOGICAL FALLACIES?

Logical fallacies are commonly known features of an argument that either demonstrate incorrect usage of logic to arrive at the conclusion or are intended to distract the reader by bringing up irrelevant information.

WHY SHOULD ARGUMENTS AVOID USING LOGICAL FALLACIES?

Being able to correctly identify logical fallacies is an important component for students making valid and sound arguments, and being able to recognize logical fallacies as well as avoid using them is part of being a critical thinker. By being able to think critically, your ideas will become well thought-out and sound judgments, and your argument's claims will not be flawed but demonstrate your credibility and skills in conceptualizing, analyzing, evaluating, synthesizing, and reasoning.

When you learn to organize your thoughts and clarify your ideas with meaningful and purposeful reflection on these types of falsehoods, you maximize your ability to recognize biases in your own thinking. As a result, your process of thinking should improve to a higher standard of fairness, credibility, accuracy, and relevance in your reasoning.

Now, while there are well over a hundred fallacies out there, you are not expected to memorize each one. Instead, the most common types have been listed below for you. To make things easier to remember, fallacies can often be divided into a number of broad categories to narrow down their type so that clear patterns can be identified, and the charts will help you understand the different patterns of faulty reasoning.

(Note: In the charts, the Latin name is listed on the left, where appropriate. Often both names are acceptable with common usage, but always check the wording of an assignment in case your instructor requires the usage of a particular one. In most cases, the Latin name will be Argumentum ad... as in Argumentum ad populum, or in other words, "Argument to/for X.")

False Appeals

The easiest of these to identify are often false appeals. In general, these are fallacies because the factors one is being asked to believe have **nothing to do with the logic** of the actual argument, asking you to consider your feelings or emotions over actual reasoning.

Latin Name	Appeal	Common Usage	Example
Ab auctoritate	Authority	Leadership figures, experts	"She's the leading expert in her field; she knows what she's doing."
Ad consequentiam	Consequences	Desired outcomes over evidence	"If you don't believe in this plan, you'll be miserable. So vote for it."
Ad passiones	Emotion	Personal arguments, soap opera	"But how does that make you *feel*?"
Ad baculum	Fear	Scare tactics, threats	"Don't let your children play outside; there are predators out there."
-	Flattery	Compliments, chat-up lines	"You're too intelligent to let a little thing like that bother you..."

Ad ignorantium	Ignorance	Burden of proof, knowledge gaps	"There's no evidence that I'm wrong, so I must be right."
Novitatis	Novelty	"Keeping up with the Joneses," sales	"The new Smartphone S—because the future is here."
Ad misericordiam	Pity	Excuses, melodrama	"I really need this job, or I'll be out on the streets."
Ad populum	Popularity	Statistics, votes	"85% of people are for this policy, so what's your opinion?"
Ad lazarum	Poverty	Charity, attacking the rich	"What does the CEO know about pain? He made $1 million this year!"
Ab absurdo	Ridicule	Comedy, sarcasm	"Honestly, my opponent is as insane as he is laughable."
Ad odium	Spite	Exploiting bitterness or bad memories	"I'd listen to him, but those nasty people have let me down before."
Ad antiquitatem	Tradition	Cultural traditions, habits	"Well, we've always done things this way, so that's the best decision."
Ad crumenam	Wealth	Bribery, greed, investments	"You should totally do it; you'll be rich!"
-	Wishful thinking	Luck, naively hoping for the best	"But what if it all works out after all?"

Evasions/Distractions

Often quite similar to the appeals above, these arguments try to convince you to consider some factor other than the content argument. Like false appeals, these try to get you to consider something other than the argument, but they focus less on the reader's **feelings** or **emotions** about the matter and more on some **external** factor. Again, there are many of these, but here is a sample.

Latin Name	Evasion/Distraction	Common Usage	Example
-	Association	Guilt by association, friendships	"He's always hanging out with those frat guys, so he must be a jerk."
-	Chronological snobbery	Backward people, social evolution	"Back then, those people were useless, barely living in huts."
-	Conspiracy theory	Cover-ups, being "in on it"	"Of course, you deny it; that just shows how manipulative they are!"
-	Genetic fallacy	Questioning origin of information	"Well, the report would say that; it came from North Korea."
Tu quoque	Hypocrisy	"You too!," attacking consistency	"You can't be against capitalism; you own a laptop and cell phone!"
Ad hominem	Personal attack	Insults, attack ads	"What a loser! I can't believe we're listening to this moron."
Ignoratio elenchi	Red herring	Missing the point, getting off topic	"Murder is bad. Oh, and speaking of murder, I could kill for a burger."
Ad infinitum	Repetition	Commercials, nagging	"I've already said it a hundred times, so aren't you convinced?"
-	Straw man	Misrepresenting an opposing side	"Now that I've explained my opponent's point; let's look at the flaws."
-	Misleading vividness	Shock ads, artistic license	"We need seat belts. I saw a gory crash today, blood everywhere!"

Generalizations

These often feature in arguments that misuse a given sample or quantity of evidence, either jumping to conclusions that are not warranted or **oversimplifying** a much more complex situation. Again, there are many of these, but here is a sample. *Continued*

Latin Name	Generalization	Common Usage	Example
Post hoc	After, therefore, because	Coincidence, reading into patterns	"The phone rang just before the power outage. I don't trust phones."
-	Biased sample	Selective surveys, loaded statistics	"The world needs more candy. Our survey (of 500 six-year-olds) said so!"
-	Cherry picking	Considering only the bits you like	"Looking at only these patients, we can see that the drug works."
-	Either/or analogy	Two choices, black-and-white thinking	"Either you're for the newspaper, or you're against it."
-	False analogy	Making inaccurate comparisons	"Running the military is like running a football team."
Secundum quid	Hasty generalization	Too little evidence for a conclusion	"Well, our first five respondents said no. Looks like we failed."
-	Moving goalposts	Requirements move after being met	"A real man does dishes. Oh you do dishes? Well, a real man would…"
-	Overwhelming exception	Exceptions ruin the generalization	"Well, apart from the stairs, rooms, and hallways, the house is fine!"
-	Single cause	Assuming one cause instead of many	"Look at all the effects caused by John running for president!"
Dicto simpliciter	Sweeping generalization	Ignoring exceptions or situations	"All the people who live in Canada are polite."

Logical Errors and Other Fallacies

This is a very broad category, but it largely consists of arguments in which the person has made <u>errors</u>, jumps in <u>logic</u>, or otherwise shows poor **reasoning** in arriving at his or her conclusion.

Latin Name	Logical Errors	Common Usage	Example
Petitio principii	Begging the question	Assuming what you're trying to prove	"I have a right to choose, so you should allow me to decide."
- (*)	Broken window fallacy	Ignoring opportunity costs/ downsides	"Destruction is profitable; it keeps the funeral homes in business."
-	Composition	Applying individual qualities to a group	"All of you are very smart, so we have a brilliant group."
-	Division	Applying group qualities to individuals	"There is baking soda in this delicious cake. Baking soda is tasty!"
-	Equivocation	Using two meanings for the same word	"This bowl is very bright, so it must be intelligent."
-	Hedging	Changing your claim to avoid counters	"Okay, when I said all cats are sneaky, I obviously only meant tigers."
Non sequitur	It does not follow	Premises don't lead to conclusion	"Following this argument for free tuition, we should go to war!"
-(*)	Naturalistic fallacy	Going from "is" to "ought" statements	"Humans have a sex drive, so we should be able to act on our urges."
-(*)	Moralistic fallacy	Going from "ought" to "is" statements	"It is wrong to cheat, so therefore, it is unnatural."
-(*)	Slippery slope fallacy	Taking the first step will lead to decline	"Legalizing drugs will lead to ten-year-olds with heroin."

Note: Some of these are debatable, marked with a (*).

There are many other fallacies out there, and indeed, several of them might overlap different categories or have debatable usage. The point though is to get used to the idea of what makes good reasoning, what pieces make up a valid or logical argument, and what information should be ignored. Hence, you will practice identifying logical fallacies in the following activity, which will improve your skills in detecting and avoiding logical fallacies.

Practice Activity E: In academia, to become a stronger critical thinker, you should be able to recognize logical fallacies. Identify which of the logical fallacies listed below appear in each of the statements and then explain briefly why each one is flawed and, as a result, invalidates any argument's claims.

A. Hasty generalization
B. Sweeping generalization
C. Begging the question
D. Red herring
E. *Post hoc* fallacy

F. *Non sequitur*
G. Either/or reasoning
H. False analogy
I. Appeal to flattery

J. *Argument ad populum*
K. *Ad hominem*
L. *Ab auctoritate* (false authority)

1. Like Thomas Edison's innovative ways, Justin Bieber was inventive in his music and vocals, but no one seemed to appreciate this young genius.
2. The majority of American parents support Obamacare.
3. Barbara Smith, a recognized expert in mathematics, argues that the objectification of women in advertising causes low self-esteem in teenage girls.
4. People who live in Chicago are mobsters.
5. Teachers are either too strict or too demanding.
6. Carol is the best mother; she would make the best governor of our state.
7. My roommate just moved in this morning, and when I got home from work tonight, my laptop was broken, so he must have done it.
8. The fact is that criminals who are sentenced to a US prison are too far delinquent to be rehabilitated.
9. From the way the two police officers pulled their guns on the two African-American boys in hoodies and not the white man holding up the liquor store in the security camera footage, we can presume that the entire police department is corrupt and racist.
10. We are all smart enough to see the drawbacks of starvation diets, given the difficulties in keeping the weight off permanently with such an unhealthy approach.
11. Dr. Mary McMurray, who earned her medical degree from Harvard, was arrested for shoplifting back in high school, so you shouldn't let her perform surgery on you or even listen to her advice after your checkup.
12. "Hey, it's time for bed," Tanya said, but her little brother Nicky begged, "But wait, can you tell me how can I know for sure if a girl likes me at a school?"

CHAPTER 5
ANALYSIS

Figure 5.1   Irony Analysis Cartoon

In this chapter, you will learn to apply analytical-thinking skills to write an argument in which you are able to carefully consider the separate components of an object, concept, event, or behavior and determine its meaning, relevancy, and function. In other words, you will be able to examine a particular item by a classification or standard, such as a theory, principle, theme, or definition. Afterward, you will be asked to put this analytical technique into practice through a set of activities.

ANALYSIS

WHAT IS ANALYSIS?

Analysis means an evaluative type of response to a poem, short story, play, or novel by examining the theme, characters, plot, symbols, irony, setting, genre, style, structure, and so forth. It can also explore historical, political, social, or philosophical works by studying them from a theoretical, critical, and rhetorical perspective. Other kinds of artistic expression and genres may include music, movies, TV shows, commercials, advertising, comic books, and video games, and they can be evaluated for their persuasive strategies as well.

WHERE CAN YOU FIND AN ANALYSIS?

To locate analysis, look no further than college essay exams, in which students must demonstrate their understanding and ability to analyze a text by using specific concepts and definitions; lab reports, in which you must assess the results of an experiment; and process analysis, in which the parts or stages of a process are divided into easy-to-understand steps. Moreover, analysis is a major part of research papers because students must incorporate theories and make connections between ideas as they examine information from their sources, while a literary analysis paper involves the study of a literary work for the imagery, symbols, characterization, plot, or other elements.

Analysis is also used in the workplace for writing grant proposals by addressing the issues behind the need for the funding and in reviews of the arts when commenting on the artistic value of a work. Likewise, in medical charts, doctors and nurses track patients' symptoms and decide on the best treatment for their recovery; in legal briefs, lawyers dissect the facts and link past legal rulings to the new circumstances, and case studies may outline the issues behind a business, medical, advertising, or social service lawsuit. Finally, business plans utilize analysis when they describe their profits, expenses, and other costs and endeavor to forecast future earnings and overheads.

HOW DO YOU WRITE AN ANALYSIS?

In order to write an analysis, consider the purpose of your investigation and ask: What is the main idea, theme, theory, criteria, principle, or definition motivating the study of this source material? This is the "So what?" question to help you establish the classification or standard by which to judge the object. Then, assess the meaning (What does this mean?), relevance (Why is this valuable or significant?), and function of the object (How does this work?).

Once you have addressed those questions by summarizing the main ideas, you should assert an argument. You may want to break it down into two parts before you formulate the thesis statement. In the first aspect of your claim, the argument consists of a standard "A" point that can refer to a theory, principle, theme, or definition, while the second component of the claim can involve a more specific element of your theory, principle, theme, or definition. See the examples below.

- **CLAIM 1**: Standard A (criteria A, theory A, theme A, principle A, definition A, etc.) is B (beneficial, ethical, valuable, moral, etc.).

    Example: Raising the minimum wage is valuable.
    Example: The theory of relativity is indispensable.

- **CLAIM 2:** By applying standard A (criteria A, theory A, theme A, principle A, definition A, etc.), one can understand (the subject: B)_____as (or use *through*, *in*, etc.)_____ (conclusion drawn from the analysis: C)_____.

> **Example:** By analyzing the objectification of women in advertising, one can understand the rise in teenage girls' eating disorders, addictions, and low-esteem as a result of these sexualized and violent images.
>
> **Example:** By analyzing the feminist theories in Charlotte Perkins Gilman's "The Yellow Wallpaper," one can understand the theme of oppression through the characters, symbols, and setting.

After you have stated an argument for your thesis, organize the essay into separate body paragraphs under the standards in which you plan to evaluate the item by logically classifying the validity or authority of the principle, theory, theme, element, or definition. Support your analysis of the object with logical claims, accurate evidence, and fact-based answers to address the investigative question that gives your analysis purpose. Finally, provide a deeper understanding of the analyzed item (i.e., issue, theme, concept, object, behavior, or event) in your conclusion, and reiterate the main points of your analysis along with the relevance, meaning, and function of the item in terms of the principle or definition examined. See the sample outline below.

Example Analysis Paper Outline

I. **Introduction** (aim for 5-7 sentences)
   A. Provide an overview of a problem or investigative question along with a summary of the issue, event, or behavior.
   B. Formulate an argument into a clear thesis statement.
II. **Body paragraph 1** (aim for 7-9 sentences): Identify the object and the first criteria, principle, or definition to form the basis of the analysis.
   A. Provide an example: Quote or paraphrase evidence.
   B. Explain the meaning, relevance, and relationships between ideas.
III. **Body paragraph 2** (aim for 7-9 sentences): Identify the object and the second criteria, principle, or definition to form the basis of the analysis.
   A. Provide an example: Quote or paraphrase evidence.
   B. Explain the meaning, relevance, and relationships between ideas.
IV. **Body paragraph 3** (aim for 7-9 sentences): Identify the object and the third criteria, principle, or definition to form the basis of the analysis.
   A. Provide an example: Quote or paraphrase evidence.
   B. Explain the meaning, relevance, and relationships between ideas.
V. **Conclusion** (aim for 5-7 sentences)
   A. Offer a deeper understanding of the theme and elements analyzed.
   B. Reiterate the main points of your essay.

WHAT ARE SOME TYPES OF ANALYSIS?

An analysis may include a rhetorical, social, or literary approach. On the one hand, a rhetorical analysis encourages a closer reading of a text, and as a result, you become a better thinker. Through the evaluation process of rhetorical analysis, you address the strategies of persuasion

Steps for Writing an Analysis:

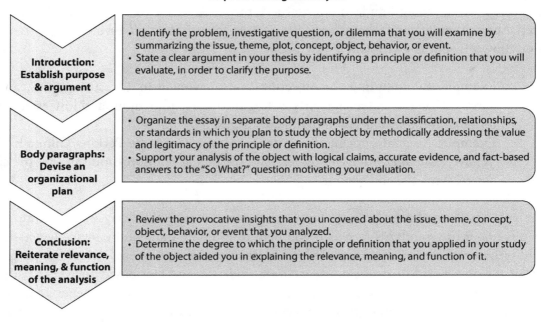

Figure 5.2

within a text and mine it for evidence to support your claims. You will most likely select many quotes as evidence in a rhetorical analysis as you respond to a specific argument by offering reasons for agreeing or disagreeing with an author or the source material.

Conversely, a social analysis is the practice of systematically examining a social problem, issue, or trend, often with the aim of encouraging changes in the situation being analyzed, while a literary analysis explores different genres, styles, themes, characters, symbols, irony, and so forth in a novel, play, poem, or short story. However, this type of analysis will force you to take a deeper look at the use of language and definitions of literary terms applied in a text. It may also prompt you to ask more provocative questions. In other cases, you may dissect a film, music, TV show, ads, comic book, or video game in a similar manner and discover other cultural, social, economic, political, philosophical, and historical influences by making associations. See the examples below.

Rhetorical Analysis Paragraph Example

By analyzing the principles behind the American Dream in Martin Luther King's "I Have a Dream" speech, one better understands the value attributed to life, liberty, and the pursuit of happiness and the need for every individual to have these unalienable rights through the rhetorical devices that he applies. For example, Martin Luther King uses the rhetorical technique of *conduplicatio* effectively when he repeats "I have a dream" throughout his speech in order to emphasize his stance for peace, unity, and equality for all without race, class, or gender restrictions. For example, he moves readers with his main argument: "I have a dream that one day this nation will rise up and live out the true meaning of its creed: 'We hold these truths to be self-evident, that all men are created equal'" (King). In other words, he envisions a world of equality for everyone as stated in the Declaration of Independence. He also includes parallelism to produce an engaging rhythm that maintains the audience's interest, such as, "We will be able to work together, to pray together, to struggle together, to go to jail together, to stand up for freedom together . . ." (King) or the lyrical language of his prose when he integrates alliteration in certain lines like the following: "Rise from the dark and desolate . . . the marvelous new militancy . . . trials and tribulations . . ." (King). Here, the "d's," "m's," and "t's" create a musical flow, unity, and coherence just like his references to "together" and "we" throughout the speech. In addition, he refers to the figurative language of the metaphorical table of brotherhood and the "heat of oppression" that may become an "oasis of freedom" for the implied metaphor of Mississippi as a desert (King). Along with these techniques, King's speech directs the readers to his allusions of "Five score years ago, a great American . . . signed the Emancipation Proclamation" and "My Country, 'Tis of Thee" and "Free at Last" to strike an emotional chord in the audience (King). In the end, one is swayed by the impassioned petition that he makes about the American Dream through his use of rhetorical devices because one can agree that everyone holds these rights sacred for themselves, their children, and future generations as he sheds light on the shared aspirations of everyone in achieving the American Dream.

Literary Analysis Paragraph Example

By analyzing the theme of pride and revenge in "The Cask of Amontillado" by Edgar Allan Poe, it becomes evident that the main character and narrator, Montresor, demonstrates these two themes in his opening confession as well as in the family crest and motto. For instance, in the first few lines of the story, he announces to the reader that he is seeking vengeance against Fortunato, who has wronged him countless times. Montresor states, "The thousand injuries done to me by Fortunato I bore as best I could. But when he insulted me, I swore I would get revenge" (Poe). Montresor admits that he wants retribution for every slight, insult, and injury that Fortunato has done to him. However, the question arises of what these injuries could possibly be that warrant reprisal, and Montresor provides an answer to the reader. According to John Gruesser, an expert on Edgar Allan Poe and professor at Kean University,

> Fortunato is the golden boy, "rich, respected, admired, beloved . . . happy . . ." [while] Montresor has not been so blessed, or as he asserts, he once was, but has lost his status and/or his contentment. To someone who is unfortunate, like Montresor, Fortunato's happiness is a daily injury. Thus, Montresor conceives and executes an ingenious plan, which appears to succeed, for revenging himself on fortune's friend. Sealed in the Montresor family vaults, Fortunato is deprived of everything. (129)

By entombing Fortunato in the vaults, Montresor believes Fortunato will finally be denied his status, wealth, and privileged lifestyle, and thus, Montresor will no longer have his pride hurt in having lost his status and enduring Fortunato's arrogance in possessing happiness, prosperity, and luck. Moreover, Montresor shows that he still has pride in his noble background and status when he identifies his family coat of arms and motto to Fortunato. Montresor tells him, "Nemo me impune lassecit! - No one attacks me with impunity!" (Poe). In other words, he warns Fortunato that no one harms him unpunished or ever gets away with it without revenge from his end.

Practice Activity A: Follow the directions below for each separate practice analysis paragraph.

1. Watch a commercial for any political candidate from the Museum of the Moving Image, *The Living Room Candidate: Presidential Campaign Commercials 1952-2012* Web site that you choose from the following link: www.livingroom candidate.org/ and write a rhetorical analysis paragraph by exploring a principle or other criteria used in the speech. (Note: You can view the transcripts of the words and credits next to each video in order to quote and cite it accurately.)

    a. Open with a topic sentence that identifies the principle, issue, event, behavior, or definition under study as well as the title and speaker that you will be analyzing in this paragraph.
    b. Introduce the speaker or author before the quotes that you include.
    c. Quote evidence from the commercial or speech in order to support your analysis of the principle or other criteria used in the speech as you suggest the meaning and relevance of the issue, concepts, events, or behavior being discussed.
    d. Explain the ways in which the commercial or speech demonstrates the principle or other criteria that you examined and share your insights and reasons for why you agree or disagree with the ideas presented in this speech and why the speaker makes a persuasive argument or why he does not.
    e. Aim to write 5-9 sentences and include at least two quotes in your paragraph.

2. Read "The Grasshopper and the Ants" by Aesop and write a literary analysis paragraph by exploring the theme of discipline versus idleness through the characters of the grasshopper and the ants.

    a. Open with a topic sentence that identifies the theme and characters as well as the title and author that you will be analyzing in this paragraph.
    b. Introduce the speaker or author before the quotes that you include.
    c. Quote evidence from the story in order to support your analysis of characters displaying discipline versus idleness.
    d. Explain the ways in which characters demonstrate the theme of discipline versus idleness and the purpose behind the lesson to be learned by examining the quote's meaning and relevance in supporting your claims.
    e. Aim to write 5-9 sentences and include at least two quotes in your paragraph.

Continued

"The Grasshopper and the Ants" by Aesop

One bright day in late autumn a family of Ants were bustling about in the warm sunshine, drying out the grain they had stored up during the summer, when a starving Grasshopper, his fiddle under his arm, came up and humbly begged for a bite to eat.

"What!" cried the Ants in surprise, "haven't you stored anything away for the winter? What in the world were you doing all last summer?"

"I didn't have time to store up any food," whined the Grasshopper; "I was so busy making music that before I knew it the summer was gone."

The Ants shrugged their shoulders in disgust.

"Making music, were you?" they cried. "Very well; now dance!" And they turned their backs on the Grasshopper and went on with their work.

There's a time for work and a time for play.

WHAT ARE SOME EXAMPLES OF AN ANALYSIS ESSAY?

Two student essays follow with practice activities for class discussion, to be done before your instructor asks you to write an analysis paper. Please read the social analysis paper, titled "Animal Testing Should Be Banned," and the literary analysis paper, titled "The Knowledge of Economic Inequality in Toni Cade Bambara's 'The Lesson.'" Then, complete each practice activity by addressing the questions.

Practice Activity B: Read the student sample of a social analysis paper, titled "Animal Testing Should Be Banned," that follows, and address the questions listed below in complete sentences in order to help you understand how a social analysis is written.

1. What is the thesis of the essay and purpose of the student's analysis? Identify the standard or principle motivating the student's analysis.
2. What argument is the student trying to make about the debatable social issue, and what did you learn from this student's analysis of it? Summarize the author's claims that give you a deeper insight on the author's argument.
3. What type of evidence is used as support for the author's thesis, and does he or she support the thesis with relevant evidence for each point/reason? Why or why not? Provide at least one example passage used as support in each of the body paragraphs being analyzed and why it is pertinent.
4. Fill out the template outline with complete sentences to help you understand the format and structure of a social analysis paper.

Continued

Template Outline

I. Introduction
   A. Provide an overview of the investigative question or topic being analyzed: _____.
   B. List the thesis statement: _____.

II. Body paragraph 1: List the topic sentence from the essay that identifies the standard and first criteria being analyzed: _____.
   A. Provide an example from the essay (quote the evidence): _____.
   B. Explain the meaning, relevance, and relationships between ideas: _____.

III. Body paragraph 2: List the topic sentence from the essay that identifies the standard and the second criteria being analyzed: _____.
   A. Provide an example from the essay (quote the evidence): _____.
   B. Explain the meaning, relevance, and relationships between ideas: _____.

IV. Body paragraph 3: List the topic sentence from the essay that identifies the standard and the third criteria being analyzed: _____.
   A. Provide an example from the essay (quote the evidence): _____.
   A. Explain the meaning, relevance, and relationships between ideas: _____.

V. Conclusion
   A. Reiterate the main points of the essay: _____.
   B. Identify the provocative insight offered from the essay: _____.

5. What's the pattern that you notice in each paragraph that makes the analysis a successful one when you consider the author's stance and three points/reasons?

Animal Testing Should Be Banned
Student Sample: Social Analysis Paper

With people's increased reliance on advanced medical technology and cosmetic products, animals are used more in testing currently than ever before. According to one study, in the United States alone, "The 2013 USDA Annual Report of Animal Usage documented 85,325 animals that experienced unrelieved pain and distress in fiscal year 2013" (Stokes 1297). Many of these animals are not being treated with the respect and dignity that they deserve. Frequently, these animals are kept locked away and subjected to a wide variety of medicines and treatments that often leave many of them scarred or suffering from other horrific side effects. On top of that, many of the tests done on animals are not even that effective, and a number of better options exist out there. By banning animal testing, the government would end the inhumane treatment of many animals, promote experimentation methods that are more compatible on human beings, and encourage the use of better alternatives.

The first reason to ban animal testing is because it is fundamentally inhumane. Many of the animals kept locked up in these labs are frequently subjected to cruel and often painful experiments that cause them to suffer, and this barbaric practice needs to be made illegal. Wendy Higgins, a writer for the *Animals' Agenda*, describes the effects of some of these horrific experiments:

Last February the commission published proposals for a new EU chemicals testing policy that relies heavily on immensely cruel toxicity tests on such animals as fish, rats, rabbits, and dogs. These animals will be forced to inhale toxic substances, have chemicals injected into their bloodstream, pumped into their stomach, spread across their shaved and abraded skin, and squirted into their eyes. Fish will have pollutants poured into their water, and pregnant animals will be poisoned to see what mutations develop in their unborn offspring. The chemical poisoning will result in painful sores, burns, internal bleeding, organ damage, cancerous tumors, muscle spasms, nausea, collapse, coma, and eventually death. (13)

This report clearly shows that many animals within these labs are not treated with the respect and dignity that they deserve, which ultimately leads to their needless suffering and even death. Therefore, animal testing should be banned because the animals are not treated properly inside of testing labs.

The second reason why animal testing needs to be banned is because many of the experiments are actually ineffective, as human physiology is not compatible with that of many animals. In fact, in many cases, while a certain medicine or drug is effective on rats or monkeys, it has proven to have radically different results when applied to human beings, making such experiments not only cruel but ultimately useless. In a paper written in the *Journal of Nursing Law,* one author explains, "Animal bodies and their systems react very differently from humans. In fact, animal tests and human results are the same only 5% to 25% of the time. Eighty-eight percent of doctors agreed that animal experiments can be misleading 'because of anatomical and physiological differences between animals and humans'" (Stachura 148). This study highlights some of the difficulty with "translating" experiments done on animals and applying them to humans, because the different physiology makes the findings of these studies inconclusive. This is why animal testing should be banned, as conducting the experiments on animals is often incompatible with human physiology.

The final reason why animal testing needs to be banned is because many better alternatives now exist. Technological developments, such as in vitro data and computer simulated models, have meant that many animal testing practices are becoming increasingly redundant. One medical report notes that there are already efforts underway in the US to create a particular resource which "aims to determine a compound's safety earlier in the drug discovery process by comparing its molecular characteristics to a database of around 3,000 pharmaceutical compounds and 7,000 environmental chemicals with known toxicity profiles" (Dolgin 1348). Using this database, scientists can avoid testing on animals when the toxicity and side-effects have already been successfully catalogued, which enables them to determine a product's safety much earlier on in the development process. This shows how other methods besides cruel animal experimentation can still produce valuable results, so animal testing should be banned to help push for adoption of these methods while enabling people to continue to create life-saving medicines.

In conclusion, animal testing should be banned because it promotes the cruel treatment of animals, it "translates" poorly to human physiology, and a number of more humane alternatives now exist. Firstly, animal testing simply fails to treat animals with the respect and dignity they deserve. Secondly, with the key differences between people and animals, many experiments on animals simply produce no useful results for human beings. Finally, many other alternatives to animal testing now exist, and society should be doing more to promote their usage instead of callous and outdated methods. Over time, society could see a real advantage in the abolition of these cruel and inhumane practices and still find real tangible gains for human beings in developing medical research, so people should do all they can to incentivize companies to move in this direction for everybody's benefit.

Works Cited

Dolgin, Elie. "Animal Testing Alternatives Come Alive in US." *Nature Medicine*, vol. 16,

no. 12, 2010. *ProQuest,* doi.org.ezproxy.library.csn.edu/10.1038/nm1210-1348.

Higgins, Wendy. "Harmful If Swallowed." *Animals' Agenda*, vol. 22, no. 1, 2002.

ProQuest, doi.org.ezproxy.library.csn.edu/10.4103/1995-705X.81548.

Stachura, Sheree. "Drug Safety: An Argument to Ban Animal Testing." *Journal of Nursing

Law*, vol. 12, no. 4, 2008. *ProQuest,* search.proquest.com.ezproxy.library.csn.edu/doc

view/206506555?accountid=27953.

Stokes, W. S. "Animals and the 3Rs in Toxicology Research and Testing." *Human and

Experimental Toxicology*, vol. 34, no.12, 2015. *ProQuest,* doi.org.ezproxy.library.csn.

edu/10.1177/0960327115598410.

Practice Activity C: Read the student sample literary analysis, titled "The Knowledge of Economic Inequality in Toni Cade Bambara's 'The Lesson,'" that follows, and address the questions listed below in complete sentences in order to help you understand how a literary analysis is written.

1. What is the thesis of the essay and purpose of the student's analysis? Identify the theme and the object motivating the student's analysis.
2. What type of evidence is used as support for the thesis, and does the author support his or her thesis with relevant evidence? Why or why not? Provide at least one example passage used as support in each of the body paragraphs for the theme and object being analyzed and state why it is pertinent.
3. Fill out the template outline to help you understand the format and structure of a literary analysis paper.

Template Outline

I. Introduction
   A. Provide an overview of the investigative question or topic being analyzed: _____.

   B. List the thesis statement: _____.

II. Body paragraph 1: List the topic sentence from the essay that identifies the object and the first criteria being analyzed: _____.
   A. Provide an example from the essay (quote the evidence): _____.
   B. Explain the meaning, relevance, and relationships between ideas: _____.

III. Body paragraph 2: List the topic sentence from the essay that identifies the object and the second criteria being analyzed: _____.
   A. Provide an example from the essay (quote the evidence): _____.
   B. Explain the meaning, relevance, and relationships between ideas: _____.

IV. Body paragraph 3: List the topic sentence from the essay that identifies the standard and the third criteria being analyzed: _____.
   A. Provide an example from the essay (quote the evidence): _____.
   A. Explain the meaning, relevance, and relationships between ideas: _____.

V. Conclusion
   A. Reiterate the main points of the essay: _____.
   B. Identify the provocative insight offered from the essay: _____.

4. What's the pattern that you notice in each paragraph that makes the author's analysis a successful one when you consider the theme and elements being analyzed?
5. What argument is the student trying to make about the story, and what did you learn from this student's analysis of it? Summarize the story in a sentence and the author's claims that give you a deeper insight.

The Knowledge of Economic Inequality in Toni Cade Bambara's "The Lesson"
Student Sample Paper: Literary Analysis

In the short story "The Lesson," Toni Cade Bambara illustrates the knowledge of economic inequality in society that an underprivileged girl named Sylvia gains when she is taken on a trip with a group of her friends to the toy store FAO Schwarz in Manhattan. While she is shown the expensive merchandise of a microscope, sailboat, and paperweight, Sylvia is provoked to consider the disparity between the poor and rich classes by Miss Moore. Miss Moore who is an educated woman takes it upon herself to teach the young and help them question social injustice. Hence, at the end of the story, Sylvia acquires this new insight but tries to resist her newfound class consciousness of the inequity in the world since it challenges everything she knew before that day. Her emotions demonstrate that she has developed an awareness of class struggle after making the connections intended by Miss Moore's lesson. The knowledge of economic inequality is the theme conveyed through the symbolism of the microscope, paperweight and sailboat in the story.

The knowledge of economic inequality is shown through the symbolism of the microscope that represents the tool of truth and inquiry. Since it magnifies hidden secrets from the naked eye, Miss Moore's trip and guided questions expand their consciousness of social injustice. Just as a microscope is used for magnifying and evaluating something, it enables the children to assess their financial limitations, thereby allowing them to realize economic inequity exists between the "have" and "have-nots" in society. When one of the children, nicknamed Big Butt, expresses a desire to buy the scientific instrument to "look at things," Miss Moore explains that he could view thousands of bacteria in a drop of water and countless other living things in the air that are normally invisible (Bambara 378). She emphasizes the unlimited possibilities that he could have if he had access to it, but this metaphorical lens is aimed at the world when she asks

them to notice the price tag of $300 for the microscope. Afterward, Miss Moore asks how long

it would take him to save his allowance for it, and Sylvia answers the question with "too long

. . . outgrown it by that time" (Bambara 378). In this example, Sylvia reminds them that time

is fleeting, but ironically, the microscope is also used to magnify the truth that the children are

unequal to the wealthy and overwhelmingly too poor. Being poor emphasizes that knowledge

is out of reach for them since the microscope represents the tool to access education, truth, and

enlightenment away from the burden of ignorance that comes with poverty. Thus, Miss Moore

gives them the intended knowledge by lifting the veil from their eyes as Sylvia demonstrates

that she has gained insight on the monetary disparity between the classes and the way in which

opportunities pass as fast as the time.

Along with the microscope, the paperweight is another symbol used to illustrate the

knowledge of economic inequality, and it signifies the weight of poverty that holds them down.

For example, Sylvia even wonders to herself about this "chunk of glass cracked with something

heavy, and different-color inks dripped into the splits, then the whole thing put into an oven or

something. But for $480 it [the paperweight] don't make sense" (Bambara 378). She admits that

she is unfamiliar with this object's use as much as the price bewilders her. Hence, when one of

the children asks what it is, Miss Moore explains, "It's to weigh papers down so it won't scatter

and make your desk untidy" (Bambara 378). Her explanation of this pretty, decorative object is

also one of function if you have the livelihood of the wealthier classes. However, Junebug claims

that she does not have a desk while Big Butt says that he does not even have homework, and by

these statements, the paperweight, essentially, adds to the children's consciousness of their own

inequality because it not only emphasizes the lack of importance that is placed on education in their lives, but it also demonstrates the poor education the children *receive* by way of the poverty they live in. Economic inequality thus effectively holds them down as a paperweight would hold down a document. The children are then able to recognize this reality through their own assertions that they would not be able to use a paperweight for anything, and they grow closer to the consciousness of class disparity through the reference to the paperweight.

Besides the paperweight, the sailboat is also a symbol used to portray the knowledge of economic inequality as the theme of the story. The expensive sailboat at FAO Schwarz represents the strong foundation of the rich to stay buoyant in life through economic independence in contrast to the poor children's homemade paper boats that embody the flimsy foundation of their world and financial insecurities in their family's lives. In fact, the children admit to Miss Moore that they make their boats with 50 cents worth of dime store materials, and it sails as a far as the string that they tie to it will let them pull it in a local park's pond until it eventually sinks (Bambara 379). The resources available to them for their sailboat implies that they are limited in getting far in life with the "string" or ties that hold them back in their poor lives. The flimsy foundation of their homemade sailboats and lives cannot keep them afloat in the world against the currents of life's small or large ponds. Instead, like the homemade sailboats, they can drown just as easily under the burden of their poverty. On the other hand, when the children read the description of the fancy, toy sailboat as "Hand-crafted sailboat of fiberglass at one thousand one hundred ninety-five dollars," Sylvia blurts out, "Unbelievable" and confesses that "this pisses me off" (Bambara 379). Her angry reaction shows that her consciousness of the economic injustice is hard to swallow, but Miss Moore's lesson is also understood by others like Sugar who sums up the group's sentiments when she says, "I think…this is not much of a democracy if you ask me. Equal chance to pursue happiness means an equal crack at the dough, don't it?" (Bambara

381). Sugar addresses the class bias and economic disparity present in society and establishes that everyone has obtained knowledge due to Miss Moore. As a result, Miss Moore's trip to the store proves to be effective in making them aware of the class divide and unfair division of wealth in society.

"The Lesson" accurately depicts the social inequality that is brought about through American wealth distributed disproportionately in society. Miss Moore guides the children to grasp the knowledge of economic inequality in the story through the use of three symbols: the microscope, the paperweight, and the sailboat. Each one is used to show the state of the injustice in the class division between the poor and rich. She helps them become consciousness of the class struggle in the U.S. by lifting the veil to see the world for what it really is. Toni Cade Bambara not only exposes the reality of poverty and inequality in America, but she challenges people to combat these truths as a society.

Works Cited

Bambara, Toni Cade. "The Lesson." *Mooring against the Tide: Writing Fiction and Poetry.*

Ed. Jeff Knorr and Tim Schell. Prentice Hall, 2001. 376-82.

CHAPTER 6
CRITIQUES

Figure 6.1   Goldilocks's Critique Gets Karma Cartoon

In this chapter, you will learn to be a better critical reader, and you will develop the skills to evaluate the validity and value of a source. When examining the rhetorical context of a source, you will be able to understand an author's purpose, credibility, and intended audience as well as discern his or her biases, expertise, and even style. In fact, you will be drawing on the information that you learned from other chapters in this textbook by utilizing summary and assessing if the source applies the appeals of argument (i.e., ethos, pathos, and logos) or if it has flawed reasoning with logical fallacies in the text or presentation.

CRITIQUE

WHAT IS A CRITIQUE?

A critique is a response to a source in which the active reader carefully considers issues and determines an educated and fair judgment of the subject's material. The active reader also approaches the source with sensitivity, inquisitiveness, creative thinking, and imagination. Moreover, the critique focuses on the facts and strategies applied by the author, and it questions the claims, evidence, and conclusions in the reading with a healthy balance between open-mindedness and skepticism.

WHERE CAN YOU FIND CRITIQUES?

To locate a written critique, look no further than academic and workplace writing. A few kinds of academic writing in which you may be required to apply critique include research papers, essay exams, book reviews, and argument papers.

For the research paper, you will prove the usefulness and credibility of sources when you evaluate them. For essay exams, you will establish your grasp of concepts and knowledge of course material by critiquing it in your responses to questions.

Similarly, in book reviews, you will combine summary with critique as you examine the reading's style, genre, purpose, and so forth. In argument papers, you pledge a stance by critiquing the opposing side's position as you demonstrate the other side's weak use of the appeals and flawed logic.

As for workplace writing, it may include business proposals, political policy briefs, and legal arguments. For instance, some business plans may evaluate the efficiency of the proposal or the expense of some intended project, while political policy briefs may share the ineffective legislation or legal arguments of a counsel's prior case ruling.

HOW DO YOU WRITE A CRITIQUE?

In order to write a critique, you must pose key questions about the reading or presentation, and then you will be able to judge it with a critical eye on the author's purpose; the use of the appeals for logos, ethos, and pathos and logical reasoning; and the extent to which you agree or disagree with the author. Here are the criteria to follow:

Criteria One: Author's Purpose

- What is the author's purpose? To inform, persuade, or entertain?
- Does the author succeed in this purpose? Why or why not?

If the author's intention is to inform, he or she will provide facts, figures, definitions, historical context, anecdotes, and other background information; if the aim is to persuade, the author will defend a position about a debatable issue by stating a clear assertion. The author will also support his or her claims by arguing logically, using information fairly, and defining terms clearly. In other words, you should ask yourself "So what?" to determine why this information is important or how it may or may not advance your knowledge of the subject.

However, if the author's target is to entertain, the reading may move you to laughter, reflection, or an emotional response because it is a good poem, play, short story, novel, film, essay, or speech. As a result, you will be able to judge the portrayal of a character, theme, plot, style, genre, irony, hyperbole, understatement, metaphors, similes, personification, repetition, and other figurative language and elements of literature.

Criteria Two: Appeals and Reasoning

- How does the author use the appeals of ethos, logos, and pathos?
- Does the author avoid emotionally loaded language and logical fallacies?

If the author is applying ethos, logos, and pathos, he or she will include information and sources that are trustworthy, accurate, up-to-date, and relevant, as well as cite facts, statistics, and authorities on the subject that will establish his or her legitimacy. Even though the author may evoke a powerful emotion, empathy, or a call to action from readers by using an emotional tone or capturing moving stories of tragic events and people, he or she will still aim to be fair and unbiased, establish expertise, and use language and syntax appropriate for the audience's needs. Moreover, the author will steer clear of using logical fallacies and will interpret information impartially.

Criteria Three: Agreement versus Disagreement

- To what extent do you agree with the author's writing or presentation of key points? Why?
- To what level do you disagree with the author's writing or presentation of key points? Why?

If the author's presentation or writing coincides with your position on the issue, you will review the reasoning behind it and offer support with evidence for its validity and value. Likewise, if you disagree with the author's views fully or to some degree, you must underscore his or her lack of focus, clarity, or reasoning. You will draw attention to the author's shortcomings and juxtapose the differences between ideas while answering the "why" with legitimate proof for the refutation or concession of the author's argument.

WHAT ARE THE STEPS TO WRITING A CRITIQUE?

Composing a critique means that you will apply the criteria discussed in this chapter. For the introduction, start by establishing the topic and author's purpose that you intend to cover. Include any background material, biographical information, or controversy behind the subject matter as well as aid readers in recognizing the significance of the reading or presentation. Along with this overview in your introduction, state a thesis with the author's position and the key points that you plan to refute or concede.

Next, write the body paragraphs of your critique. For example, your first body paragraph may need to summarize the author's objectives in his or her presentation of idea or intention for writing the piece. Highlight the author's key points and the significance of his or her reasoning. Once the context of the source material is determined in the first body paragraph, the second body paragraph should evaluate the author's credibility or unreliability and fairness or bias, and then the clarity of his or her information, definition of terms, and success at accomplishing his or her goals.

You will most likely examine three key areas, such as the accuracy and relevance of the information, the author's use of appeals (i.e., ethos, logos, and pathos), and the author's approach to arguing logically. The third body paragraph involves your reaction or response to the author's views. You will address the areas in which you are in agreement or disagreement and the reasons for your position. Besides this approach, you should aim to connect the author's reasons to your own deductions about the source material and include convincing evidence.

Finally, the conclusion paragraph should reiterate the main points of the author's view, purpose, and success at meeting his or her intentions, and then recap your response to the author's position. You should direct the readers to understand the strengths or weaknesses of the source as you emphasize the insights gained about the source material and author's trustworthiness, knowledge, and poignancy in your critique's concession or refutation of the author's standpoint.

Example Critique Outline

I. **Introduction** (aim for 5-7 sentences)
   A. Provide an overview of author's purpose, background material, biographical information, and/or controversy behind the topic.
   B. Formulate a thesis statement with the author's position and key points that you intend to refute or concede.
II. **Body paragraph 1—Summary** (aim for 7-9 sentences): Identify the author's objectives in the presentation and intentions in his or her piece.
   A. Summarize author's key points and cite information: Quote or paraphrase evidence.
   B. Explain the meaning, relevance, and relationship between the author's ideas.
III. **Body paragraph 2—Evaluation** (aim for 7-9 sentences): Identify the author's credibility, fairness, clarity, definition of terms, and success at accomplishing his or her goals.
   A. Provide three examples of the author's argument and stance: Quote or paraphrase evidence.
   B. Explain the meaning of the author's views, use of appeals (i.e., ethos, logos, and pathos), and approach to arguing logically.
IV. **Body paragraph 3—Response** (aim for 7-9 sentences): Identify the author's views that you hold in agreement or in disagreement as well as the reason for your position.
   A. Provide an example: Quote or paraphrase evidence to make concessions or refute the author's ideas.
   B. Explain the meaning of the author's views and connect his or her reasoning to your own deductions about the source material and why you refute or concede the author's views.
V. **Conclusion** (aim for 5-7 sentences)
   A. Offer a deeper understanding of the key points and elements discussed.
   B. Reiterate the main points of your essay.

Steps for Writing a Critique:

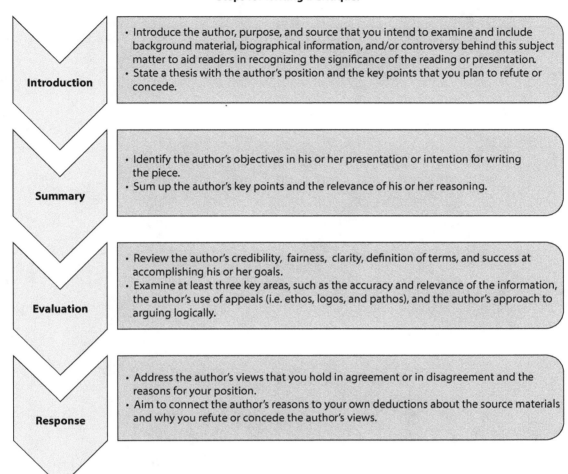

Introduction
- Introduce the author, purpose, and source that you intend to examine and include background material, biographical information, and/or controversy behind this subject matter to aid readers in recognizing the significance of the reading or presentation.
- State a thesis with the author's position and the key points that you plan to refute or concede.

Summary
- Identify the author's objectives in his or her presentation or intention for writing the piece.
- Sum up the author's key points and the relevance of his or her reasoning.

Evaluation
- Review the author's credibility, fairness, clarity, definition of terms, and success at accomplishing his or her goals.
- Examine at least three key areas, such as the accuracy and relevance of the information, the author's use of appeals (i.e. ethos, logos, and pathos), and the author's approach to arguing logically.

Response
- Address the author's views that you hold in agreement or in disagreement and the reasons for your position.
- Aim to connect the author's reasons to your own deductions about the source materials and why you refute or concede the author's views.

Figure 6.2

Practice Activity A: Write a critique of a political ad from a specific campaign year; you can select a Democratic or Republican candidate's ad from the link provided below:

- Aim to write approximately 500-750 words when you use the structure discussed in this chapter to organize your critique in five paragraphs.

- Discuss the logical fallacies that the author uses to persuade his or her audience and/or the appeals of logos, ethos, and pathos in terms of making a convincing argument.

- Provide a full citation in MLA format to credit the source that you use from the following link: www.livingroomcandidate.org/.

CHAPTER 7
SYNTHESIS

Figure 7.1   Synthesis Cartoon

In this chapter, you will learn to integrate sources in a written discussion and determine which sources, ideas, and information best suit your purpose. You will also apply many of the skills that you developed from other chapters, such as summarizing, paraphrasing, quoting, analyzing, and critiquing sources. However, you will exceed your previous proficiency in these areas since you will be looking at relationships between two or more sources rather than just an individual source.

Before you can draw information from primary or secondary sources, you will need to understand them by using summary, and then you will want to take the next step in making judgments through critical reading or the critique approach that you applied in the previous chapter. You will essentially deduce the value and authority of sources and whether you agree or disagree with the ideas covered in the sources. In fact, you will learn to discern why you agree or disagree with them.

SYNTHESIS

WHAT IS SYNTHESIS?

A *synthesis* is a written explanation, argument, or comparison and contrast that combines two or more sources in a meaningful way. You may draw material from articles, books, journals, graphs and tables, laboratory data, studies, music samples, cartoons, photographs, illustrations, artwork, and your own independent ideas. You will pull the information together in some kind of harmony to serve your purpose, theory, or thesis. In other words, you will report on the facts and new knowledge gained through research and by applying a thesis-driven approach when you organize your ideas.

In most cases, you will record your findings through multiple methods, such as summary, analysis, comparison, and evaluation, without solely relying on any particular tool. In other words, a synthesis is not a summary of your sources but is more in line with writing a shorter research paper in which you qualify, defend, or challenge an argument or claim. By developing a position and evaluating several features and sources related to the topic, you will make insightful connections when you show the relationship between two or more works and why these perspectives are important.

WHERE CAN YOU FIND A SYNTHESIS?

Synthesis is used in academic and workplace writing in several ways. For essay exams, you may be asked to compare and contrast hypothesis, concepts, and premises in order to show your comprehension of course materials. Similarly, most argument papers synthesize different viewpoints in support of a particular stance in order to make a persuasive case from convincing evidence found in the sources. While research papers integrate various types of sources, an analysis paper tends to incorporate theoretical, critical, and rhetorical perspectives from different sources in its evaluation of a criteria, theme, principle, or definition.

Workplace writing may include business plans, memos, and letters that synthesize policies, events, and proposals for a unified sharing of information, while Web sites attach a variety of links and related information from multiple sources. Policy briefs take a compare-and-contrast approach since they must determine the best course of action in resolving a crisis or other challenges, while newspapers and magazines integrate sources to report their findings with fact-based studies, firsthand accounts, and other data as evidence.

HOW DO YOU WRITE A SYNTHESIS?

Since there are three main types of synthesis—explanatory, argumentative, and compare and contrast—you will need to consider what approach best serves your purpose. With the explanatory synthesis, your purpose is mainly to inform, so your focus tends to be more objective in presenting the facts or opinions of the source rather than the writer's interpretation of ideas. Hence, you will summarize key points from sources rather than interpreting their ideas.

For example, you may be explaining a historical event as you recount where, when, and how it occurred, but you will need to draw from source materials and integrate them in your paper's discussion. By reporting the facts and citing evidence from sources, you maintain legitimacy when you select sources that serve your purpose and support your thesis, since you are not challenging values or questioning policies in order to persuade an audience. Instead, your discussion explains an event, activity, or interest or the meaning of a policy, theory, or philosophy, and so forth. Consider the example explanatory synthesis thesis and outline that follow.

- **Thesis:** Playing RPG video games has been linked to improved cognitive-thinking skills, enhanced hand-eye coordination, and reduced stress.

  I.   Introduction: Provide overview and thesis.
  II. First point (i.e., cognitive-thinking skills improved) summarized with supporting evidence from a source.
  III. Second point (i.e., hand-eye coordination enhanced) summarized with supporting evidence from a source.
  IV. Third point (i.e., stress reduced) summarized with supporting evidence from a source.
  V.   Conclusion: Reiterate the main points discussed.

Unlike the explanatory synthesis, the argumentative serves to persuade, so its thesis is a claim in which you assert a stance or propose a course of action that you aim to prove. You aim to provide evidence from facts and reliable experts to support this claim. The connection between the supporting evidence and claim is your assumption (or warrant) about the subject or issue. In other words, as discussed in previous chapters, the assumption (or warrant) is the core belief that you hold about some aspect of an issue and how it works.

You will create an outline and organize your essay from claims and assumptions as well as supporting evidence from sources. Your argument strategy should also employ the three appeals of logos, ethos, and pathos as discussed in previous chapters. Argue logically, demonstrate credibility, and move your readers' emotions as you persuade them with the information that you will present. Here is an example of an argumentative thesis and a possible outline format.

- **Thesis:** Preventing the legalization of prostitution undermines the potential to reduce the spread of STDs, avert violent crimes against sex workers, and raise tax revenue for the community's benefit.

  I.   Introduction: Provide overview and thesis.
  II. Discuss the first claim and an assumption (preventing the legalization of prostitution undermines the potential to reduce the spread of STDs) and prove it through supporting evidence from sources.
  III. Discuss the second claim and an assumption (preventing the legalization of prostitution undermines the potential to avert violent crimes against sex workers) and prove it through supporting evidence from sources.
  IV. Discuss the third claim and an assumption (preventing the legalization of prostitution undermines the potential to raise tax revenue for the community's benefit) and prove it through supporting evidence from sources.
  V.   Conclusion: Reiterate main points of your argument.

Similar to the argumentative synthesis, the compare-and-contrast synthesis will be persuasive in nature. There are two basic ways to organize your key points: by criteria and by source or subject. For organizing by criteria, discuss two sources concurrently as you examine the views of each author point by point (criterion by criterion). This approach works best when you have several relevant key points to discuss or when the subject is highly complex and passages are quite long.

Basically, you will go back and forth between the two sides as you make connections for each point or criteria, but you should direct the audience toward your answer for the "So what?" question before the end of your synthesis, since you should strive to make an argument. Here is an example of a compare-and-contrast synthesis as well as organizing by criteria:

- Although college students are opposed to campus speech codes, the board of education argues that such codes prevent discrimination against race, gender, and sexual orientation.

  I.   Introduction: Provide overview of comparison and state thesis.
  II. Criterion 1 (reason or point 1 on the prevention of racial discrimination with speech codes): Compare one author's reasons to another author's points and quote or paraphrase evidence.
  III. Criterion 2 (reason or point 2 on the prevention of gender discrimination with speech codes): Compare one author's reasons to another author's points and quote or paraphrase evidence.
  IV. Criterion 3 (reason or point 3 on the prevention of sexual orientation discrimination): Compare one author's reasons to another author's points and quote or paraphrase evidence.
  V.   Conclusion: Reiterate the key points of your comparison.

You may choose to apply organizing by source or subject, in which you summarize one source at a time with the objective of comparing them later instead of simultaneously, like you do for organizing by criteria. After you review the features of one subject or source, familiarize your audience with the other subject or source.

Then, follow with a discussion about their similarities and differences as you make connections between them. This approach is better suited for shorter passages or simpler subjects that can be reviewed in brief highlights, and again, the answer to "So what?" should be addressed by the time you approach your conclusion. Here is an example of organizing by source or subject and a potential thesis.

- **Thesis:** Despite the government's argument that gun control is necessary to reduce crime in communities, many Americans are opposed to the hindrance of their Second Amendment rights to protect their family's safety if a gun ban occurred in the United States.

  I.   Introduction: Provide an overview of the debate and state a thesis.
  II. Summarize source/subject A: Highlight its most relevant characteristics and quote or paraphrase evidence (i.e., government argues gun control reduces crime in communities).
  III. Summarize source/subject B: Highlight its most relevant characteristics and quote or paraphrase evidence (i.e., Americans argue gun control hinders their Second Amendment right to protect their family's safety).
  IV. Discuss the major points of comparison and contrast between the sources or subjects: Compare one source's reasons to another source's as you provide evidence by quoting or paraphrasing from the source material.
  V.   Conclusion: Reiterate the main points of the comparison.

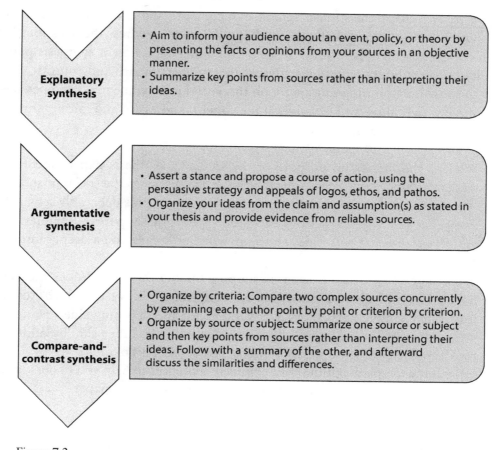

Figure 7.2

WHAT IS AN EXAMPLE OF A SYNTHESIS?

You will read an example of a student compare-and-contrast synthesis paper that builds from a previous topic and paper (analysis), in order to show you how synthesis and analysis are interlinked in writing college-level argument essays that are supported with sources. There is a practice activity that corresponds to the reading that asks you to address several questions to help you understand why this student's compare-and-contrast synthesis paper was successful in making a claim and assumption with a thesis, providing a balanced discussion for the opposing sides, synthesizing evidence from credible sources, and including a refutation or concession for the other side in the paper's discussion.

Practice Activity A: Read the student sample of a compare-and-contrast synthesis paper, titled "Animal Testing Should Be Banned," that follows, and address the questions listed below in complete sentences in order to help you understand how a synthesis paper is written. Note how it builds from the analysis paper to the compare-and-contrast synthesis essay to show the opposing side's view on this social issue while making a persuasive case for one side over the other. Consider if the paper is successful and fair in refuting or conceding to the counterarguments discussed.

1. What is the thesis and purpose of the student's synthesis paper? Identify the student's stance and the reasons that he or she discusses the social problem.
2. What argument is the student trying to make about this debatable social issue, and what did you learn from this student's synthesis paper? Summarize the author's claims for both sides and state whether it gave you a deeper insight on this social issue.
3. What type of evidence is used as support for the thesis, and does the author have a fair and balanced discussion for both sides? Why or why not? Provide at least one example passage used as support for the opposing side's paragraphs and address if the author refutes or concedes to the other side by addressing logical fallacies or the appeals of logos, ethos, and pathos.
4. Fill out the template outline with complete sentences to help you understand the format and structure of a compare-and-contrast synthesis paper.

Template Outline

I. Introduction
    A. Provide an overview of the investigative question or topic being analyzed: _____.
    B. List the thesis statement: _____.

II. Body paragraph 1: List the topic sentence from the essay that identifies the author's stance and first reason/criteria: _____.
    A. Provide an example from the essay (quote the evidence): _____.
    B. Explain the meaning, relevance, and relationships between ideas: _____.

III. Body paragraph 2: List the topic sentence from the essay that identifies the opposing side's view for the first reason/criteria: _____.
    A. Provide an example from the essay (quote the evidence): _____.
    B. Explain the meaning, relevance, and relationships between ideas and how the author refutes or concedes to the other side: _____.

IV. Body paragraph 3: List the topic sentence from the essay that identifies the author's stance and second reason/criteria: _____.
    A. Provide an example from the essay (quote the evidence): _____.
    B. Explain the meaning, relevance, and relationships between ideas: _____.

Continued

V. Body paragraph 4: List the topic sentence from the essay that identifies the opposing side's view for the second reason/criteria: _____.
   A. Provide an example from the essay (quote the evidence): _____.
   B. Explain the meaning, relevance, and relationships between ideas and how the author refutes or concedes to the other side: _____.

VI. Body paragraph 5: List the topic sentence from the essay that identifies the author's stance and third reason/criteria: _____.
   A. Provide an example from the essay (quote the evidence): _____.
   B. Explain the meaning, relevance, and relationships between ideas: _____.

VII. Body paragraph 6: List the topic sentence from the essay that identifies the opposing side's view for the third reason/criteria: _____.
   A. Provide an example from the essay (quote the evidence): _____.
   B. Explain the meaning, relevance, and relationships between ideas and how the author refutes or concedes to the other side: _____.

VIII. Conclusion
   A. Reiterate the main points of the essay: _____.
   B. Identify the provocative insight offered from the essay: _____.

5. What's the pattern that you notice in each paragraph that makes the compare-and-contrast synthesis paper a successful argument on this social issue?

Animal Testing Should Be Banned
Student Sample: Compare-and-Contrast Synthesis Paper

With people's increased reliance on advanced medical technology and cosmetic products, animals are used more in testing currently than ever before. According to one study, in the United States alone, "The 2013 USDA Annual Report of Animal Usage documented 85,325 animals that experienced unrelieved pain and distress in fiscal year 2013" (Stokes 1297). Many of these animals are not being treated with the respect and dignity that they deserve. Frequently, these animals are kept locked away and subjected to a wide variety of medicines and treatments that often leave many of them scarred or suffering from other horrific side effects. On top of that, many of the tests done on animals are not even that effective, and a number of better options exist out there. However, opponents argue that experimenting on animals is necessary for developing essential medicines along with the fact that there are several benefits to animal testing and that few viable alternatives are available. By banning animal testing, the government would end the inhumane treatment of many animals, promote experimentation methods that are more compatible on human beings, and encourage the use of better alternatives, although the opposing side disagrees with these reasons and stance.

The first reason to ban animal testing is because it is fundamentally inhumane. Many of the animals kept locked up in these labs are frequently subjected to cruel and often painful experiments that cause them to suffer, and this barbaric practice needs to be made illegal. Wendy Higgins, a writer for *The Animals' Agenda*, describes the effects of some of these horrific experiments:

Last February the commission published proposals for a new EU chemicals testing policy that relies heavily on immensely cruel toxicity tests on such animals as fish, rats, rabbits, and dogs. These animals will be forced to inhale toxic substances, have chemicals injected into their bloodstream, pumped into their stomach, spread across their shaved and abraded skin, and squirted into their eyes. Fish will have pollutants poured into their water, and pregnant animals will be poisoned to see what mutations develop in their unborn offspring. The chemical poisoning will result in painful sores, burns, internal bleeding, organ damage, cancerous tumors, muscle spasms, nausea, collapse, coma, and eventually death. (13)

This report clearly shows that many animals within these labs are not treated with the respect and dignity that they deserve, which ultimately leads to their needless suffering and even death. Therefore, animal testing should be banned because the animals are not treated properly inside of testing labs.

However, the other side argues that even though many of these animals are not treated humanely, it is a necessary evil to develop valuable new medicines. Rachel Hajar, who works at the Department of Cardiology and Cardiothoracic Surgery at Hamad Medical Corporation, discusses how "total elimination of animal testing will significantly set back the development of essential medical devices, medicines, and treatment" (42). Her article goes on to explain how prior to animal testing, many drugs and medicines were tested on human beings, often with disastrous and fatal results. This evidence indicates that if animal testing were to be banned, many valuable medications and products could not have been developed, and even though many animals suffer horrific side effects, it is still better than human beings suffering instead. Thus, opponents argue that animal testing should not be banned because society needs it to develop valuable medications and treat a number of different illnesses. On the whole though, this is a weak argument because it uses the false dilemma fallacy, arguing that either society permits inhumane treatment of animals, or it lets human beings suffer instead. In many cases, there is simply no reason why animals cannot be treated better in these labs, even if animal testing is allowed to continue for the purpose of developing quality medications and life-saving treatments.

The second reason why animal testing needs to be banned is because many of the experiments are actually ineffective, as human physiology is not compatible with that of many animals. In fact, in many cases, while a certain medicine or drug is effective on rats or monkeys, it has proven to have radically different results when applied to human beings, making such experiments not only cruel but ultimately useless. In a paper written in the *Journal of Nursing Law,* one author explains that, "Animal bodies and their systems react very differently from humans. In fact, animal tests and human results are the same only 5% to 25% of the time. Eighty-eight percent of doctors agreed that animal experiments can be misleading 'because of anatomical and physiological differences between animals and humans'" (Stachura 148). This study highlights some of the difficulty with "translating" experiments done on animals and applying them to humans, because the different physiology makes the findings of these studies inconclusive. This is why animal testing should be banned, as conducting the experiments on animals is often incompatible with human physiology.

On the other hand, opponents of this view explain that while the results of the experimentation done on animals cannot always be applied to human beings, it is still valuable for expanding our base of scientific knowledge. Only rarely does the testing on animals yield no practical benefit whatsoever, and indeed many of these studies have actually benefitted human beings in many subtle ways, as one report examines, "Testing chemicals on animals helps protect human health. For example, studies have indicated that frogs and rats suffer adverse effects from pesticides such as atrazine, diazinon, and Dursban. Animal test results led to the banning of these products by the Environmental Protection Agency" (Solomon 48). Here one can see that there are many practical advantages to animal testing that do not necessarily depend on how applicable the test results are to direct development of medicines, so the other side would argue that animal testing should not be banned because it still produces a number of useful benefits in growing our scientific knowledge. However, again this is a fairly weak argument, as it uses the Red Herring fallacy. If the primary purpose, and indeed the justification, of animal testing is to apply these medicines to human beings, then the fact that doing these experiments produces other tangible "side-benefits" is irrelevant when considering the primary reason to conduct testing on animals. Even if the experiments do produce other valuable results, this does not address the fact that the main reason for doing them in the first place is ultimately flawed.

The final reason why animal testing needs to be banned is because many better alternatives now exist. Technological developments, such as in vitro data and computer simulated models, have meant that many animal testing practices are becoming increasingly redundant. One medical report notes that there are already efforts underway in the US to create a particular resource which "aims to determine a compound's safety earlier in the drug discovery process by comparing its molecular characteristics to a database of around 3,000 pharmaceutical compounds and 7,000 environmental chemicals with known toxicity profiles" (Dolgin 1348). Using this database, scientists can avoid testing on animals when the toxicity and side-effects have already been successfully catalogued, which enables them to determine a product's safety much earlier on in the development process. This shows how other methods besides cruel animal experimentation can still produce valuable results, so animal testing should be banned to help push for adoption of these methods while enabling people to continue to create life-saving medicines.

In contrast though, opponents would argue that while many of the alternatives to animal testing exist, in particular cases, these other methods are either too expensive or too impractical to be put into widespread usage. While these technological developments might be useful to avoid needless animal suffering, the fact that they involve expensive equipment and are limited in scope prevents scientists from simply applying them in every situation. In particular, an extensive research report conducted by the *Archives of Toxicology* asserts that there are a number of issues with the in vitro proposed alternative to animal testing. They say, "To reconstruct all human tissues, in vitro would be a formidable task today, and toxicological testing on all separate tissue models would put even the direst estimates of animal use in a temporally and economically favorable light" (Liebsch et al. 844). One can see here that these alternatives have very clear limitations, and that while promoting them might be idealistic, it is fundamentally not that realistic. This is a fairly strong argument that makes a convincing logos appeal, as the opponents explain with clear facts and evidence that alternatives to animal testing have their limits.

In conclusion, animal testing should be banned because it promotes cruel treatment of animals, it "translates" poorly to human physiology, and a number of more humane alternatives now exist, even though opponents would still disagree with this view. Overall, animal testing simply fails to treat animals with the respect and dignity they deserve, and although some might argue it is a necessary evil to produce valuable medicines for human beings, there is no justification for not treating the animals properly in order to do it. Furthermore, since there are key differences between people and animals, many experiments on animals simply produce no useful results for human beings, and despite opponents might argue that there are other side benefits to continuing testing, it should be minimized to only important medical research, rather than in the production of consumer cosmetic goods. Finally, as many other alternatives to animal testing now exist, even if these are often impractical or expensive, society should be doing more to promote their usage, such as expanding both research and funding in these areas. Over time, society could see a real advantage in the abolition of these cruel and inhumane practices and still find real tangible gains for human beings in developing medical research, so people should do all they can to incentivize companies to move in this direction for everybody's benefit.

Works Cited

Dolgin, Elie. "Animal Testing Alternatives Come Alive in US." *Nature Medicine*, vol. 16,

no. 12, 2010. *ProQuest,* doi.org.ezproxy.library.csn.edu/10.1038/nm1210-1348.

Hajar, Rachel. "Animal Testing and Medicine." *Heart Views,* vol. 12, no. 1, 2011. *ProQuest,*

doi.org.ezproxy.library.csn.edu/10.4103/1995-705X.81548.

Higgins, Wendy. "Harmful If Swallowed." *Animals' Agenda*, vol. 22, no. 1, 2002. *ProQuest,*

doi.org.ezproxy.library.csn.edu/10.4103/1995-705X.81548.

Liebsch, Manfred, et al. "Alternatives to Animal Testing: Current Status and Future

Perspectives." *Archives of Toxicology,* vol. 85, no. 8, 2011. *ProQuest*, doi.org.ezproxy.lib

rary.csn.edu/10.1007/s00204-011-0718-x.

Solomon, Gina. "Chemical Testing on Animals Saves Lives." *Animal Experimentation*. Ed.

Cindy Mur, Greenhaven Press, 2004, 47-49.

Stachura, Sheree. "Drug Safety: An Argument to Ban Animal Testing." *Journal of Nursing

Law*, vol. 12, no. 4, 2008. *ProQuest,* search.proquest.com.ezproxy.library.csn.edu/docview/

206506555?accountid=27953.

Stokes, W. S. "Animals and the 3Rs in Toxicology Research and Testing." *Human and

Experimental Toxicology*, vol. 34, no.12, 2015. *ProQuest*, doi.org.ezproxy.library.csn.edu/

10.1177/0960327115598410.

CHAPTER 8
RESEARCH

Figure 8.1   The Three Stages of Research Grief Cartoon

In this chapter, you will learn about the fundamentals of doing research and composing a research paper. Foremost, you will understand the importance of posing a challenging question to help guide your research, exploring the library and Web for sources, and evaluating source materials on how current, credible, and relevant they are.

You will draw on many of the skills developed in previous chapters, like assessing the value of your sources and synthesizing them into your paper's discussion. However, you will also be able to create an annotated bibliography, in order to determine the types of sources and evidence you have collected. As a result, you will organize your information more efficiently and effectively to avoid plagiarism. You will also have the opportunity to practice the features reviewed in this chapter with some activities.

RESEARCH

WHAT IS RESEARCH?

Research means gathering data, navigating various library databases or the Web to locate sources, or even conducting your own studies, experiments, and interviews. It also means joining the academic conversation of scholars, because your initial steps include finding a topic by posing a sophisticated question on a debatable issue, for instance, and then narrowing your focus to something manageable and accessible.

WHERE IS RESEARCHED WRITING FOUND AND USED?

Different types of researched writing can be found in many fields in the workplace as well as in the academic arena. For example, you may be called on in your job to write a business plan or market analyses that require data, while others may be asked to produce scientific, medical, or engineering reports by conducting experiments or surveys and collecting facts and other statistical information.

There is also legal research applied toward a court case, and similarly, in academia, position papers, research-based essays, and literature reviews cite relevant studies and sources in support of an argument. Case studies might draw on personal accounts for primary sources and secondary research, but experimental reports may include trials and other testing in their gathering of information.

HOW SHOULD YOU START YOUR RESEARCH?

To start your research, ask an initial question on a topic that fits the guidelines of your assignment. This question will be the driving force in finding appropriate sources before you develop a working thesis. If your preliminary question is too broad, you may need to revise it and limit it to a clearer focus, or if it speculates on a subject that can easily be answered with a yes or no, then you will need to articulate a different question that will direct you to plenty of information and sources that can help you be more selective in winnowing it down to the most pertinent material. Here are some examples of questions that are too broad:

- **Weak question:** What causes Alzheimer's?
- **Weak question:** Where is 3-D printing being used?

Instead, you will want to revise your question to be more focused and challenging, but most importantly, it should be grounded in credible, relevant, and up-to-date evidence, not just opinions, such as the following:

- **Strong question:** How has the use of over-the-counter anticholinergic drugs been linked to cognitive impairment and an increased risk of dementia?
- **Strong question:** What makes 3-D printing of human organs and body parts medically and economically feasible?

WHAT APPROACH WILL HELP YOU FIND SUITABLE SOURCES IN THE LIBRARY AND ON THE WEB?

In order to find suitable sources, consider the types of sources that will benefit your paper as well as meet the requirements of the assignment. You may want to explore your local or college library database and consult a reference librarian, who can help you focus your search. If your library search produces too many prospective source materials, you may need to restrict the options to more current publications or even limit them to a specific type of source, such as an article in a popular nonacademic magazine versus a peer-reviewed scholarly journal.

Search the library catalogs and databases with keywords for your topic. For example, if you are trying to locate sources on "over-the-counter anticholingergic drugs" because you heard they were linked to cognitive impairment and the risk of dementia, and this does not yield much information, you may need to try alternative names. For example, you may want to type: "antimuscarinic agents" or "antinicotinic agents."

Moreover, if the assignment requires you to use primary or secondary sources, you should understand the difference between them. Primary sources involve your own original materials, such as interviews, case studies, surveys, laboratory observations, and fieldwork that you have personally recorded or conducted. Secondary sources examine and explain the information in primary sources; these include scholarly journals and books, government reports, or reviews in newspapers and magazines.

You may want to use the Web as well, and filter your search for more sophisticated sources with other options, such as using **double quotation marks** (" ") when you type keywords in lowercase to locate both lower- and uppercase versions of your topic. Typing capitalized letters usually returns only an exact match. Therefore, you would place (" ") around the words as you type them, not just around a single word, in order to produce an exact search, such as "Poet Laureate 1970."

You may want to include specific **anchor** phrases to help expand your search as well. You would list descriptive words for the exact term, separate these modifier phrases with commas, and even add a larger date range when you type everything in the search engine to produce more results: racial minority, women, "Poet Laureate" 1970 . . . 2015.

Another handy option is **a plus sign (+)** and **a minus sign** (-) before phrases. In other words, if you want to require certain phrases in your search in order to refine your search to be inclusive of specific documents, place a plus sign (+) before your term. This will ensure that all of your source materials contain the correct words: inventions +Tesla.

However, if you desire your search to remove certain words and exclude documents from appearing with those terms, put a minus sign (-) in front of phrases: cardinals -football -Arizona. (There should be no space between the sign and keywords). As a result, the results will omit everything that has to do with football and Arizona for this specific search.

In addition, you may apply the **Boolean operators,** such as **AND, OR, NOT,** and parentheses ( ), since each of these insertions allow for excluding and requiring words, and other complex combinations of words. When you do a search and you include AND, it is the same as putting a plus sign (+) in front of the words, so documents must contain all of the words coupled together with the AND operator: Citizen AND Kane AND movie.

Inserting the **OR operator** produces documents that contain at least one of the words connected with OR, as in the following: dog OR puppy. Attaching the **AND operator** is similar to the plus sign (+), and the **NOT operator** means the exact same thing as applying the minus sign (-) in front of words. As a result, your search will only produce documents that do not contain the word after the term AND NOT, such as the following: revolvers AND NOT Colt Python. The other alternative to apply includes **parentheses** ( ) if you intend to group portions of your Boolean queries simultaneously; for example, to locate documents that have the word *vegetables* and either the words *carrots* or *peppers* in them, you might enter: vegetables AND (carrots OR peppers).

Finally, there are search techniques, known as **wildcards, truncation,** or **stemming,** that permit symbols, such as a question mark (?) or asterisk (*), to stand in for missing letters. You can search for variants of terms, such as library*, and the search will return alternatives in spelling and word form: library, libraries, librarian, etc. However, despite the usefulness of these different search strategies, there are downsides to each of them from time to time, and you may need to vary your application of them to have the most successful outcomes.

HOW SHOULD YOU EVALUATE YOUR RESEARCH SOURCES?

You should evaluate a research source by determining if it is relevant to your topic. In other words, does it offer evidence in support of your stance, or does it provide an unconventional perspective to enhance your understanding of the subject even if you disagree with it? The source may also help you refute the other side's argument by helping you consider the opposing position, or it may strengthen your paper's discussion by answering your research question with facts and legitimate information.

Questions to Ask to Check for Relevance

- Does the source provide facts, data, and statistics to establish background information?
- Does the source provide counterarguments, new perspectives from the opposition, or evidence to support your assertions?
- Does the source provide explanations of concepts and clarification for the meaning of definitions?

Then, decide if it is a trustworthy and reliable source. To resolve if a source is actually credible, you should read about the author's background, expertise, education, and other qualifications. However, if it's a publication by an organization, you should assess the type of studies, lab observations, surveys, and data gathering that the organization might have conducted before you decide to integrate the source in your paper's discussion.

Questions to Ask to Check for Credibility

- Does the source include opposing viewpoints and treat them fairly, or are there signs of bias, such as a particular political or religious affiliation of the author that demonstrates a lack of objectivity?
- Does the source include accurate data and statistics and cite the origins of those facts?
- Does the source include the author's expertise, education, and qualifications that lend authority and shows the author's trustworthiness?

Furthermore, you will want to ensure that you have the most up-to-date sources by checking the date. If there's a more current source, there is no point in using an outdated study or report—unless you want to use it as a point of comparison between old and new trends in a specific field. Decide the purpose that the sources will serve in terms of lending authority to your claims, affording evidence for your argument, suggesting counterevidence, defining concepts and specialized terminology, and providing background information.

Questions to Ask to Check for Currency

- Does the source have the most current data and up-to-date statistics?
- Does the source cite contemporary cases, technological advancements, the latest medical references, and modern scientific studies?
- Does the source indicate information is fresh or links are updated and topical on a Web site or other forum?

HOW DOES AN ANNOTATED BIBLIOGRAPHY ASSIST IN THE RESEARCH PROCESS?

The annotated bibliography aids in the further evaluation of your sources, and since it is likely that your instructor will assign it with a specific number of sources in mind before you begin writing your paper, you will need to decide if your sources are credible, relevant, and current as discussed earlier. Creating an annotated bibliography is necessary since it will help you judge if a source is biased and unreliable or pertinent to your argument.

Read through your sources, highlight significant passages for evidence, and take notes in the margins as you gather information. Once you complete this initial step, provide citation information in MLA format, summarize the source in the present tense, and aim for your annotation to be three to seven sentences. Here is an example of an annotated bibliography entry that summarizes the author's claims and purpose to clearly identify the argument and evidence:

Harrington, Scott. "The Debate on Vaccination Safety in Our Youth." *The Autism Epidemic in America*, edited by Noah Waters and Samantha Katz. Penguin Press, 2015, pp. 183–205.

In this chapter, Dr. Scott Harrington, who specializes in pediatrics at Johns Hopkins Medical Center, argues the pro-pharma mainstream media wants parents to trust in the safety of vaccines as a preventative measure against the spread of diseases. However, his twenty-five-year study addresses the various side effects and symptoms that develop from the ingredients in hepatitis B vaccine; diphtheria, tetanus, and accellular pertussis vaccines; heamophilus influenzae type

B vaccine, inactivated poliovirus vaccine, pneumococcal conjugate vaccine, and rotavirus vaccine. He also cites other studies, statistics, and cases to show the rise in autism in the past two decades may be due to the immunization schedule that begins with infants and follows children into their teenage years.

HOW SHOULD YOU MANAGE INFORMATION FROM SOURCES TO PREVENT PLAGIARISM?

To manage your information and prevent plagiarism, it is important to document each source as you use it. Maintain a working bibliography for your sources, which means you should properly credit the sources with full citation information in MLA format. Then, as you read sources with a critical eye and select details methodically, be careful to take notes in your own words.

However, you should use the exact words of an author when quoting. In fact, you should label your notes with the source's information: author, title, publisher, page, date, URL, DOI, and so on. Afterward, you will be able to locate it again and properly credit the source when you quote, paraphrase, and/or summarize from it.

Along with documenting your sources and taking accurate notes, stay organized by saving electronic sources and creating a file on your desktop to store them. This will make it easier to retrieve and consult the source again and check that you have accurately quoted, paraphrased, and/or summarized from it. For instance, if you find an article from the library's database, you might e-mail it to yourself, download it, or save it directly onto your computer in a file that you designate for your research materials.

You may locate books in your search, and as a result, you will want to photocopy or scan a chapter and keep track of the author, title and subtitle, publication information: city, publisher, and year, and medium of publication as you make progress in finding sources and evaluating them. These extra steps will help keep you on track with your source materials as well as better organized.

WHAT IS THE KEY TO A SUCCESSFUL RESEARCH PAPER PROJECT?

Follow the guidelines discussed in this chapter to have a successful research paper project. You will need to have an initial research question, search for appropriate sources on your topic, evaluate the quality of the sources you find, create an annotated bibliography, and manage the information effectively by documenting your sources and recording the exact words of a source accurately to prevent plagiarism.

Furthermore, you need to adhere to your instructor's requirements for the assignment, which may mean providing a proposal of your topic, an annotated bibliography, and possibly a research plan before you begin writing your research paper. The proposal should state clearly and concisely what you intend to research, such as an initial question that will drive your research and the claim or argument that you intend to make. Your goal will be to prove why your research project is viable within a reasonable time frame as well as the merits of pursuing it.

Hence, your proposal should give a description of the purpose behind your inquiry on a debatable issue, social problem, or controversy. Establish your focus with an investigative question and a tentative working thesis, and then explain the knowledge that you already have about the topic and why you have chosen it. Afterward, determine a plan to conduct a search for sources via the library and on the Web, or even engage in field research, interviews, or surveys. It is beneficial to create a schedule to keep you on track and to manage your time, but there will be a practice activity to assist you in getting organized and staying on track to meet the requirements and deadline of your research paper project.

Practice Activity A: Create a research proposal, annotated bibliography, and research plan and schedule, but be sure to adhere to your instructor's requirements for the research paper as well.

1. Research proposal: Follow the steps below and create a research paper proposal.
   A. List your investigative question and your purpose for your inquiry (aim for 1-3 sentences).
   B. State a preliminary thesis with stance and reasons (aim for 1 sentence). (Note: You may need to use a template thesis if your instructor requires it.)
   C. Identify the knowledge that you already have on the topic and what you still hope to learn (aim for 1-3 sentences).
   D. Locate sources on your topic by using the techniques listed below as you search the library database as well as the Web and then list these sources with a citation in MLA format.
      1. Refine your search by applying each of these techniques when you type in your keyword search and then list at least one source that you found under each technique. Which ones produced the most useful sources, and which types had their drawbacks?
      2. Double quotation marks (" "): _____
      3. Anchor phrases: _____
      4. A plus sign (+) and/or a minus sign (-): _____
      5. Boolean operators (parentheses ( ), AND, BUT, NOT, OR): _____
      6. Wildcards, truncation, or stemming (question mark ? or asterisk *): _____

2. Annotated bibliography: Follow the steps below to create an annotated bibliography.
   A. Include citation information in MLA format for each of your sources.
   B. Summarize each source in the present tense and aim for your annotation to be three to seven sentences.

3. Research plan and schedule: Follow the steps below to create a research plan and schedule.
   A. Produce a research plan by setting at least three goals for yourself to help you stay organized as you search for sources in the library's database and Web, conduct any interviews or surveys, and begin writing your research paper.
   B. Establish a schedule with dates and deadlines for the time frame of your research project in order to stay organized and on track to meet the target date for submitting your work to your instructor.

Steps for a Successful Research Project:

Research question
- Draft a sophisticated question on a debatable issue, social problem, or controversy that will be interesting to you and your audience and be the driving force behind your research.
- Aim to pose a challenging line of inquiry with an argument that should be grounded by evidence, not just beliefs, speculations, or opinions.

Search for sources
- Search for suitable sources with keywords for your topic in the library catalogs and databases as well as the Web.
- Refine your search by applying double quotation marks, anchor phrases, a plus sign, a minus sign, the Boolean operators, wildcards, truncation, or stemming with your keyword entry.

Evaluate sources
- Evaluate the quality of your sources for being relevant, credible, and current by asking the questions listed in this chapter.
- Assess source's evidence for its pertinence to your topic in providing an unbiased expert's perspective and offering the most recent statistics and facts.

Annotated bibliography
- Determine the quality of your sources further by evaluating your sources with the annotated bibliography.
- Include citation information in MLA format, summarize the source in the present tense, and aim for your annotation to be three to seven sentences.

Prevent plagiarism
- Manage information by recording the exact words of sources and documenting them as you quote, paraphrase, and summarize from them to prevent plagiarism.
- Stay organized by labeling any notes that you take in your own words with the source's information: author, title, publisher, page range, date, URL, DOI, etc. and save electronic sources in a file on your computer or make copies that you can access easily.

Proposal & schedule
- Prepare a research proposal to include an investigative question on your topic, a tentative working thesis, knowledge that you already have about the topic, and why you have chosen this topic.
- Determine a plan and schedule to conduct a search for your sources via the library and on the Web, or engage in field research, interviews, or surveys to stay organized and meet deadlines.

Figure 8.2

WHAT IS AN EXAMPLE OF A RESEARCH PAPER?

You will read an example of a student research paper that builds from the previous papers (analysis and synthesis), and there is a practice activity that accompanies it. The activity will ask you to address several questions to help you understand why this student's research paper project was a successful one in terms of implementing a clearly stated thesis, supporting it with evidence from legitimate library sources, and crediting sources with parenthetical citations and a Works Cited page in MLA format.

Practice Activity B: Read the student sample research paper, titled "Animal Testing Should Be Banned," that follows, and address the questions listed below in complete sentences in order to help you understand how a research paper is written. Note the way in which the paper was built from the analysis and synthesis essays as the solutions on this social issue are addressed.

1. What is the thesis and purpose of the student's research paper? Identify the student's stance, the reasons discussed for both sides, and his or her solutions to this social problem.
2. What argument is the student trying to make about this debatable social issue, and what did you learn from this student's research paper? Summarize the author's claims that give you a deeper insight on the author's argument and why these solutions are viable or not.
3. What type of evidence is used as support for the author's thesis, and does he or she support the thesis with relevant evidence for the solutions in particular? Why or why not? Provide at least one example passage used as support for the paragraphs that cover the solutions.
4. Fill out the template outline with complete sentences to help you understand the format and structure of an analysis paper.

Template Outline

I. Introduction
    A. Provide an overview of the investigative question or topic being analyzed: _____.
    B. List the thesis statement: _____.

II. Body paragraph 1: List the topic sentence from the essay that identifies the author's stance and first reason/criteria: _____.
    A. Provide an example from the essay (quote the evidence): _____.
    B. Explain the meaning, relevance, and relationships between ideas: _____.

III. Body paragraph 2: List the topic sentence from the essay that identifies the opposing side's view for the first reason/criteria: _____.
    A. Provide an example from the essay (quote the evidence): _____.
    B. Explain the meaning, relevance, and relationships between ideas and how the author refutes or concedes to the other side: _____.

Continued

IV. Body paragraph 3: List the topic sentence from the essay that identifies the solution for the first reason/criteria: _____.
   A. Provide an example from the essay (quote the evidence): _____.
   B. Explain the meaning, relevance, and relationships between ideas: _____.

V. Body paragraph 4: List the topic sentence from the essay that identifies the author's stance and second reason/criteria: _____.
   a. Provide an example from the essay (quote the evidence): _____.
   b. Explain the meaning, relevance, and relationships between ideas: _____.

VI. Body paragraph 5: List the topic sentence from the essay that identifies the opposing side's view for the second reason/criteria: _____.
   A. Provide an example from the essay (quote the evidence): _____.
   B. Explain the meaning, relevance, and relationships between ideas and how the author refutes or concedes to the other side: _____.

VII. Body paragraph 6: List the topic sentence from the essay that identifies the solution for the second reason/criteria: _____.
   A. Provide an example from the essay (quote the evidence): _____.
   B. Explain the meaning, relevance, and relationships between ideas: _____.

VIII. Body paragraph 7: List the topic sentence from the essay that identifies the author's stance and third reason/criteria: _____.
   A. Provide an example from the essay (quote the evidence): _____.
   B. Explain the meaning, relevance, and relationships between ideas: _____.

IX. Body paragraph 8: List the topic sentence from the essay that identifies the opposing side's view for the third reason/criteria: _____.
   A. Provide an example from the essay (quote the evidence): _____.
   B. Explain the meaning, relevance, and relationships between ideas and how the author refutes or concedes to the other side: _____.

X. Body paragraph 9: List the topic sentence from the essay that identifies the solution for the third reason/criteria: _____.
   A. Provide an example from the essay (quote the evidence): _____.
   B. Explain the meaning, relevance, and relationships between ideas: _____.

V. Conclusion
   A. Reiterate the main points of the essay: _____.
   B. Identify the provocative insight offered in the essay: _____.

5. What's the pattern and techniques (i.e., analysis, synthesis, etc.) that you notice in each paragraph that makes the research paper a successful and persuasive one?

Animal Testing Should Be Banned
Student Sample: Research Paper

With people's increased reliance on advanced medical technology and cosmetic products, animals are used more in testing currently than ever before. According to one study, in the United States alone, "The 2013 USDA Annual Report of Animal Usage documented 85,325 animals that experienced unrelieved pain and distress in fiscal year 2013" (Stokes 1297). Many of these animals are not being treated with the respect and dignity that they deserve. Frequently, these animals are kept locked away and subjected to a wide variety of medicines and treatments that often leave many of them scarred or suffering from other horrific side effects. On top of that, many of the tests done on animals are not even that effective, and a number of better options exist out there. However, opponents argue that experimenting on animals is necessary for developing essential medicines along with the fact that there are several benefits to animal testing and that few viable alternatives are available. By banning animal testing, the government would end the inhumane treatment of many animals, promote experimentation methods that are more compatible on human beings, and encourage the use of better alternatives, although the opposing side disagrees with these reasons and stance.

The first reason to ban animal testing is because it is fundamentally inhumane. Many of the animals kept locked up in these labs are frequently subjected to cruel and often painful experiments that cause them to suffer, and this barbaric practice needs to be made illegal. Wendy Higgins, a writer for *The Animals' Agenda*, describes the effects of some of these horrific experiments:

Last February the commission published proposals for a new EU chemicals test-

ing policy that relies heavily on immensely cruel toxicity tests on such animals as fish,

rats, rabbits, and dogs. These animals will be forced to inhale toxic substances, have

chemicals injected into their bloodstream, pumped into their stomach, spread across

their shaved and abraded skin, and squirted into their eyes. Fish will have pollutants

poured into their water, and pregnant animals will be poisoned to see what mutations

develop in their unborn offspring. The chemical poisoning will result in painful sores,

burns, internal bleeding, organ damage, cancerous tumors, muscle spasms, nausea, col-

lapse, coma, and eventually death. (13)

This report clearly shows that many animals within these labs are not treated with the

respect and dignity that they deserve, which ultimately leads to their needless suffering and

even death. Therefore, animal testing should be banned because the animals are not treated

properly inside of testing labs.

However, the other side argues that even though many of these animals are not

treated humanely, it is a necessary evil to develop valuable new medicines. Rachel Hajar,

who works at the Department of Cardiology and Cardiothoracic Surgery at Hamad

Medical Corporation, discusses how "total elimination of animal testing will significantly

set back the development of essential medical devices, medicines, and treatment" (42). Her

article goes on to explain how prior to animal testing, many drugs and medicines were

tested on human beings, often with disastrous and fatal results. This evidence indicates

that if animal testing were to be banned, many valuable medications and products could

not have been developed, and even though many animals suffer horrific side effects, it is still better than human beings suffering instead. Thus, opponents argue that animal testing should not be banned because society needs it to develop valuable medications and treat a number of different illnesses. On the whole though, this is a weak argument because it uses the false dilemma fallacy, arguing that either society permits inhumane treatment of animals, or it lets human beings suffer instead. In many cases, there is simply no reason why animals cannot be treated better in these labs, even if animal testing is allowed to continue for the purpose of developing quality medications and life-saving treatments.

As a compromise then, clearly the solution to this issue would be that if animal testing were allowed to continue, it should only be done where necessary and when it can be conducted with the utmost care. Tipu Aziz, John Stein, and Ranga Yogeshwar, doctors in the Department of Neurosurgery at John Radcliffe Hospital, explain, "Although it [animal testing] is clearly a part of advancing medical science, there are times when its use is debatable. In the pharmaceutical industry, some new drugs are developed because they are expected to provide a financial pay-off, even though effective drugs for the condition in question already exist." One of the authors goes on to say that, during his previous job in a nuclear reactor, "I had an argument with one scientist because I thought that he was working in such a sloppy way that much of his data, produced at the expense of dozens of rats, meant nothing" (458). His argument is that while animal testing should be allowed, strict rules and regulations are not sufficient to guarantee the well-being of animals, and that those conducting the experiments need to be more conscientious to minimize needless suffering of other animals. By increasing awareness and education, animal testing can still be conducted for peoples' benefit, without the needless suffering of animals in routine tests that could otherwise be avoided.

The second reason why animal testing needs to be banned is because many of the experiments are actually ineffective, as human physiology is not compatible with that of many animals. In fact, in many cases, while a certain medicine or drug is effective on rats or monkeys, it has proven to have radically different results when applied to human beings, making such experiments not only cruel but ultimately useless. In a paper written in the *Journal of Nursing Law,* one author explains, "Animal bodies and their systems react very differently from humans. In fact, animal tests and human results are the same only 5% to 25% of the time. Eighty-eight percent of doctors agreed that animal experiments can be misleading 'because of anatomical and physiological differences between animals and humans'" (Stachura 148). This study highlights some of the difficulty with "translating" experiments done on animals and applying them to humans, because the different physiology makes the findings of these studies inconclusive. This is why animal testing should be banned, as conducting the experiments on animals is often incompatible with human physiology.

On the other hand, opponents of this view explain that while the results of the experimentation done on animals cannot always be applied to human beings, it is still valuable for expanding our base of scientific knowledge. Only rarely does the testing on animals yield no practical benefit whatsoever, and indeed many of these studies have actually benefitted human beings in many subtle ways, as one report examines, "Testing chemicals on animals helps protect human health. For example, studies have indicated that frogs and rats suffer adverse effects from pesticides such as atrazine, diazinon, and Dursban. Animal test results led to the banning of these products by the Environmental Protection Agency" (Solomon 48). Here one can see that there are many practical advantages to animal testing that do not necessarily depend on how applicable the test results are to direct development of medicines, so the other side would argue that animal testing should not be banned because it still produces a number of useful benefits in growing our scientific knowledge. However, again this is a fairly weak argument, as it uses the Red Herring fallacy. If the primary purpose, and indeed the justification, of animal testing is to apply these medicines to human beings, then the fact that doing these experiments produces other tangible "side-benefits" is irrelevant when considering the primary reason to conduct testing on animals. Even if the experiments do produce other valuable results, this does not address the fact that the main reason for doing them in the first place is ultimately flawed.

This is why one solution to move forward in this debate would be to limit animal testing to purely medical research, as opposed to allowing it for cosmetic purposes. While opponents would argue that numerous medical benefits can result from animal testing, the case to allow animal testing for make-up products like lipstick, mascara and even certain cosmetic surgeries is much harder to argue. In the E.U. for example, one writer at *Postmedia News* notes that animal testing has already been banned for cosmetic purposes since 2013. "The European Union's recent ban on the sale of cosmetic products and ingredients that have been tested on animals may have ripple effects across the pond... The ban, which came into effect March 11, applies in Europe to both domestically sold and imported cosmet-ics—products ranging from sunscreen to lipstick . . . " (Kofmel). Clearly this demonstrates that elsewhere in the world, people are moving toward limiting the scope of animal testing, and while conducting experiments on animals for valuable or life-saving research might be justified, conducting it for simple frivolous consumer goods is much less acceptable.

The final reason why animal testing needs to be banned is because many better alternatives now exist. Technological developments, such as in vitro data and computer simulated models, have meant that many animal testing practices are becoming increasingly redundant. One medical report notes that there are already efforts underway in the US to create a particular resource which "aims to determine a compound's safety earlier in the drug discovery process by comparing its molecular characteristics to a database of around 3,000 pharmaceutical compounds and 7,000 environmental chemicals with known toxicity profiles" (Dolgin 1348). Using this database, scientists can avoid testing on animals when the toxicity and side-effects have already been successfully catalogued, which enables them to determine a product's safety much earlier on in the development process. This shows how other methods besides cruel animal experimentation can still produce valuable results, so animal testing should be banned to help push for adoption of these methods while enabling people to continue to create life-saving medicines.

In contrast though, opponents would argue that while many of the alternatives to animal testing exist, in particular cases, these other methods are either too expensive or too impractical to be put into widespread usage. While these technological developments might be useful to avoid needless animal suffering, the fact that they involve expensive equipment and are limited in scope prevents scientists from simply applying them in every situation. In particular, an extensive research report conducted by the *Archives of Toxicology* asserts that there are a number of issues with the in vitro proposed alternative to animal testing. They say that, "To reconstruct all human tissues, in vitro would be a formidable task today, and toxicological testing on all separate tissue models would put even the direst estimates of animal use in a temporally and economically favorable light" (Liebsch et al. 844). One can see here that these alternatives have very clear limitations, and that while promoting them might be idealistic, it is fundamentally not that realistic. This is a fairly strong argument that makes a convincing logos appeal, as the opponents explain with clear facts and evidence that alternatives to animal testing have their limits.

A possible option then that both sides can probably agree on is that while alternatives to animal testing might be too expensive or not always be practical, society should be doing more to promote their use. Expanding funding for these other methods and putting more effort in research would go a long way toward phasing out cruel and ineffective animal testing over time, as well as producing real value for human beings who can enjoy the benefits of more advanced medical products as a result. One research report examining in vitro alternatives says that "alternative in vitro methods are now available and in development, and, while not currently a complete replacement for animal testing, can be used prior to, and in some cases to complement, existing techniques. With growing developments in knowledge and technology, in vitro tests should become more predictive of the in vivo situation and should be used wherever possible" (May et al. 165). Clearly this source shows that even though alternatives to animal testing are in their infancy, further development of these technologies is both possible and desirable, so expanding both funding and research in this area might make them eventually cheaper and more practical at some point in the future.

In conclusion, animal testing should be banned because it promotes cruel treatment of animals, it "translates" poorly to human physiology, and a number of more humane alternatives now exist, even though opponents would still disagree with this view. Overall, animal testing simply fails to treat animals with the respect and dignity they deserve, and although some might argue it is a necessary evil to produce valuable medicines for human beings, there is no justification for not treating the animals properly in order to do it. Furthermore, since there are key differences between people and animals, many experiments on animals simply produce no useful results for human beings, and despite opponents might argue that there are other side benefits to continuing testing, it should be minimized to only important medical research, rather than in the production of consumer cosmetic goods. Finally, as many other alternatives to animal testing now exist, even if these are often impractical or expensive, society should be doing more to promote their usage, such as expanding both research and funding in these areas. Over time, society could see a real advantage in the abolition of these cruel and inhumane practices and still find real tangible gains for human beings in developing medical research, so people should do all they can to incentivize companies to move in this direction for everybody's benefit.